Learning SAP Concur

A Complete Guide to Travel, Expense, and Invoice Management

Contents at a Glance

This outline covers key aspects of travel, expense, and invoice management, providing a comprehensive understanding of SAP Concur's capabilities.

Part I: Introduction to SAP Concur

1. **Understanding SAP Concur**
   Overview of SAP Concur and its role in streamlining business travel, expense, and invoice processes.
2. **Setting Up SAP Concur for Your Organization**
   Steps to configure SAP Concur to suit organizational needs, including account setup and user roles.
3. **Navigating the SAP Concur Interface**
   A guide to the layout, key features, and modules within SAP Concur.

Part II: Travel Management

4. **Configuring Travel Preferences**
   Setting up travel policies, preferred vendors, and integrating travel options.
5. **Creating and Managing Travel Requests**
   How to create travel requests, manage approvals, and track travel itineraries.

Part III: Expense Management

Chapter 1: Understanding SAP Concur

Introduction

SAP Concur is a leading cloud-based solution designed to simplify and automate travel, expense, and invoice management for organizations of all sizes. By centralizing these essential financial processes, SAP Concur empowers businesses to gain real-time visibility into their spending, streamline compliance, and improve overall efficiency. This chapter will provide a foundational understanding of SAP Concur, exploring its core functionalities, benefits, and the value it adds to both employees and management teams.

The Purpose of SAP Concur

In a rapidly evolving business landscape, organizations often grapple with managing travel bookings, tracking expenses, and processing invoices in a way that is both efficient and compliant with company policies. SAP Concur addresses these challenges by offering an integrated platform that consolidates all these aspects in one seamless experience.

The platform is especially beneficial for organizations that need to manage travel and expenses across multiple departments, locations, and even countries. By digitizing and automating processes, SAP Concur reduces the burden of manual data entry, minimizes errors, and allows employees to focus on higher-value tasks.

Key Components of SAP Concur

SAP Concur consists of three main modules, each catering to a specific area of business operations:

1. **Concur Travel**
   This module simplifies the travel booking process, enabling employees to book flights, hotels, and rental cars directly within the platform. Concur Travel enforces company policies by limiting travel choices to approved providers and pre-negotiated rates, ensuring both cost savings and compliance.
2. **Concur Expense**
   Concur Expense streamlines the entire expense reporting process. Employees can capture and upload receipts via mobile, link transactions to specific projects or clients, and submit reports for approval. This module automates approvals, tracks spending, and integrates with corporate credit cards, providing a clear picture of all expenses incurred.
3. **Concur Invoice**
   Concur Invoice automates invoice capture, processing, and payment. This module integrates with accounts payable to speed up vendor

payments, reducing the risk of late fees and improving vendor relationships. By digitizing the entire invoice workflow, Concur Invoice eliminates manual processing and enables real-time tracking of invoice status.

How SAP Concur Works

SAP Concur works as a cloud-based solution, which means it is accessible from anywhere with an internet connection. Employees can log into the web application or use the mobile app to manage travel bookings, submit expenses, and capture invoices. Let's explore how each module operates:

- **Travel Booking**: Employees can book flights, hotels, and other travel options through a user-friendly interface. Once a booking is completed, it automatically links to the expense report for tracking purposes.
- **Expense Capture and Submission**: Concur Expense offers several methods for capturing expenses. Employees can take photos of receipts with the mobile app, email receipts, or upload them directly. Corporate card transactions are automatically pulled into the system for easy reporting.
- **Invoice Processing**: Invoices can be submitted electronically or scanned into the system, where optical character recognition (OCR) extracts

relevant details. The invoice is then routed through an approval process and ultimately sent to accounts payable for payment.

The Benefits of Using SAP Concur

SAP Concur is designed to bring tangible benefits to organizations, enhancing efficiency, reducing costs, and improving visibility. Here are some of the key advantages:

1. **Increased Efficiency**: By automating manual processes, SAP Concur minimizes the need for repetitive tasks, speeding up workflows for employees and managers alike.
2. **Enhanced Compliance and Control**: SAP Concur enforces travel and expense policies, preventing unauthorized expenses and ensuring employees book within company guidelines.
3. **Improved Accuracy**: With automated receipt capture and integration with corporate cards, SAP Concur reduces the risk of data entry errors and ensures accurate reporting.
4. **Greater Transparency and Reporting**: SAP Concur provides real-time insights into spending patterns. Management teams can access detailed reports on travel, expense, and invoice data, enabling better budget control and financial planning.

5. **Mobile Access**: The SAP Concur mobile app allows employees to manage their travel bookings, capture receipts, and submit expenses on the go, enhancing convenience and productivity.

Real-World Applications of SAP Concur

SAP Concur is used by organizations across various industries, from small businesses to large enterprises. Below are some examples of how SAP Concur benefits different sectors:

- **Healthcare**: In healthcare organizations, employees frequently travel between facilities and conferences. SAP Concur ensures that travel and expenses are tracked accurately, adhering to industry-specific compliance requirements.
- **Education**: Educational institutions use SAP Concur to manage travel and expense budgets for faculty and staff. The solution provides transparency and accountability for public funds.
- **Manufacturing**: In manufacturing companies, SAP Concur enables better management of vendor invoices and expense tracking for site visits, making it easier to stay within budget and manage vendor relationships.

SAP Concur in the Digital Transformation Landscape

In today's era of digital transformation, companies are increasingly moving to cloud-based solutions to enhance efficiency and agility. SAP Concur aligns with this trend, allowing businesses to transition away from paper-based processes to a fully digital, automated approach.

With its real-time analytics, mobile capabilities, and integration with SAP's broader suite of solutions, SAP Concur offers a complete solution for businesses looking to modernize their travel, expense, and invoice management processes. By adopting SAP Concur, companies can embrace a forward-thinking approach, leveraging technology to drive operational improvements and build a more productive workforce.

Conclusion

This chapter has introduced you to the basics of SAP Concur, its key components, and the benefits it brings to organizations. By automating travel, expense, and invoice management, SAP Concur is an essential tool for modern businesses, helping them save time, reduce costs, and improve compliance.

In the following chapters, we will delve deeper into each module, providing you with a comprehensive guide to setting up, configuring, and maximizing the use of SAP Concur for your organization.

This detailed explanation provides readers with a clear understanding of SAP Concur's purpose, components, benefits, and practical applications in business contexts, setting the foundation for the rest of the book.

Chapter 2: Setting Up SAP Concur for Your Organization

Introduction

Setting up SAP Concur for an organization is the first critical step toward streamlining and automating travel, expense, and invoice processes. A well-configured setup aligns with company policies, simplifies workflow, and ensures that employees can easily adopt the platform. This chapter will guide you through the setup process, covering key configuration steps, user roles, policy settings, and integration options to help you get the most out of SAP Concur.

Understanding the Configuration Workflow

The SAP Concur setup involves configuring modules, setting up user roles, defining policies, and integrating with financial and ERP systems. Although it can be customized to meet specific business needs, a typical configuration workflow includes:

1. **Defining Organizational Policies and Standards**
2. **User Account and Role Setup**
3. **Module Configuration (Travel, Expense, Invoice)**
4. **Policy Enforcement Rules**
5. **Integration with ERP/Financial Systems**
6. **Testing and Employee Training**

Each of these steps will be covered in detail, so you can confidently set up SAP Concur in a way that meets your organization's requirements.

Step 1: Defining Organizational Policies and Standards

Before configuring SAP Concur, it's essential to outline the company's policies and standards for travel, expenses, and invoice processing. This includes defining:

- **Travel Policies**: Preferred vendors, expense limits, booking procedures, and approval workflows.
- **Expense Policies**: Allowable expense types, limits for specific categories, and receipt requirements.
- **Invoice Policies**: Rules for vendor selection, invoice processing timelines, and payment terms.

Clearly defined policies provide a foundation for configuring SAP Concur and ensure compliance across all levels of the organization.

Step 2: User Account and Role Setup

User roles in SAP Concur define access levels and responsibilities. For a successful setup, it's crucial to assign roles that reflect employees' responsibilities within the organization. Common roles include:

- **Administrator**: Has full control over SAP Concur's configuration and can access all data. Administrators manage settings, add users, and monitor policy adherence.
- **Manager**: Responsible for approving employee expenses and travel requests. Managers can view and approve submissions from team members.
- **Employee**: Can submit travel requests, book travel, and submit expenses. Employees have limited access and can only view their own data.
- **Accounts Payable/Finance**: Manages invoice processing, payment schedules, and financial reports within the Invoice module.

Step 3: Configuring Travel Module

The Travel module allows employees to book travel and ensures that all bookings adhere to company policies. Key steps in configuring the Travel module include:

1. **Integrating Preferred Vendors**: Set up partnerships with travel vendors (e.g., airlines, hotels) and integrate preferred options into the booking interface.
2. **Defining Travel Approval Workflows**: Decide on the level of approval required for travel bookings. For instance, all international travel requests may require an additional level of authorization.

3. **Setting Up Policy Rules**: Configure booking limits, such as maximum allowable rates for flights or hotels, blackout dates, and restrictions on certain travel options.
4. **Configuring Notifications and Alerts**: Enable notifications for travel approvals, itinerary changes, and cancellations to keep employees and approvers informed in real-time.

Step 4: Configuring Expense Module

The Expense module simplifies expense capture, submission, and reimbursement. Effective configuration of this module ensures compliance and streamlines approval processes. Key steps include:

1. **Setting Up Expense Categories**: Define categories such as meals, transportation, lodging, and miscellaneous expenses. Each category can have its own limit based on the company's policies.
2. **Configuring Receipt Requirements**: Set rules for which expenses require receipts. For instance, you may require receipts for all expenses over $25.
3. **Defining Approval Workflow**: Establish multi-level approval processes for expense reports. For example, expenses over a certain amount may require approval from both the manager and finance.

4. **Enabling Corporate Card Integration**: Link corporate credit cards to Concur, allowing transactions to flow automatically into employees' expense reports.
5. **Policy Violations and Automatic Flags**: Set up automated flags to highlight expenses that exceed policy limits or fall outside typical spending patterns.

Step 5: Configuring Invoice Module

The Invoice module allows organizations to digitize their accounts payable process, automating invoice capture and approval. Configuring the Invoice module involves:

1. **Vendor Management**: Upload or sync vendor lists to maintain consistency. SAP Concur allows linking to external vendor databases for ease of access.
2. **Defining Approval Levels**: Set approval workflows based on invoice amount or vendor type. For example, high-value invoices may require CFO approval.
3. **Invoice Capture and OCR**: Configure the system to use OCR (Optical Character Recognition) for automatically capturing data from scanned invoices.
4. **Payment Schedules and Terms**: Set payment terms based on agreements with vendors, and

configure SAP Concur to prioritize payments as needed.

5. **Integration with Accounts Payable**: Link the Invoice module with the company's accounts payable system for automated payment processing.

Step 6: Policy Enforcement Rules

Policy enforcement is key to maintaining compliance and managing costs. SAP Concur allows for detailed customization of policy rules that are automatically enforced across modules. Examples include:

- **Travel Compliance**: Enforcing booking restrictions, such as restricting business class travel for flights under a specified duration.
- **Expense Limitations**: Setting daily spending limits for meals or lodging, with automatic notifications for policy violations.
- **Invoice Approval Limits**: Ensuring that only authorized personnel can approve invoices beyond a certain threshold.

These enforcement rules can be customized to flag policy violations, ensuring that both employees and managers are aware of non-compliant actions and can take corrective action as needed.

Step 7: Integrating with ERP and Financial Systems

Integration with ERP systems, like SAP ERP or other financial software, enables a seamless flow of data between SAP Concur and the organization's financial systems. Key benefits of integration include:

- **Automated Data Sync**: Financial data from Concur automatically syncs with the ERP, eliminating the need for manual entry.
- **Enhanced Reporting**: Integration with financial systems enables comprehensive reporting, providing insights into spending patterns, budget adherence, and vendor performance.
- **Improved Financial Planning**: Real-time expense, travel, and invoice data enhances the organization's ability to forecast budgets accurately.

Step 8: Testing and Training

Testing and training are critical to the successful rollout of SAP Concur across an organization. Testing ensures that configurations align with policies, while training empowers employees to make the most of the platform.

1. **Testing Configurations**: Conduct user testing to ensure each module functions as intended. This includes verifying that approval workflows, policy limits, and integrations work smoothly.

2. **Employee Training**: Provide role-specific training to employees, managers, and finance staff. Emphasize key functionalities, such as submitting expenses, booking travel, and approving invoices.
3. **Ongoing Support**: Consider setting up a support team or help desk to assist employees with any issues that arise during the initial stages of implementation.

Common Challenges in SAP Concur Setup

Setting up SAP Concur may present certain challenges, including data migration, policy adjustments, and user adoption. Here are some tips to address these challenges:

- **Data Migration**: Ensure that existing data, such as employee information, vendor details, and policy documents, is accurately transferred into SAP Concur.
- **Policy Adjustments**: As you begin using SAP Concur, you may find that certain policies need adjustment. Regularly review and update policies based on real-world usage.
- **User Adoption**: Encourage user adoption through training, clear documentation, and responsive support. Communicate the benefits of SAP Concur to ensure employees understand how it simplifies their tasks.

Conclusion

Setting up SAP Concur is a multi-step process that involves defining policies, configuring modules, assigning roles, and ensuring compliance with organizational standards. Proper setup is essential for maximizing the benefits of SAP Concur, from streamlined processes to enhanced visibility into spending. By following this chapter's guidelines, you will be well-equipped to implement SAP Concur in a way that supports your organization's goals and improves efficiency across departments.

In the next chapter, we'll explore the configuration of the Travel module in more detail, guiding you through booking settings, approval workflows, and policy enforcement to ensure smooth travel management.

This detailed chapter offers a step-by-step approach to setting up SAP Concur, providing readers with a comprehensive understanding of the initial configuration process.

Chapter 3: Navigating the SAP Concur Interface

Introduction

Understanding the SAP Concur interface is essential for making full use of its functionalities, from booking travel and submitting expenses to managing invoices. This chapter provides a comprehensive walkthrough of the SAP Concur interface, covering each of the platform's primary sections, navigation tips, and key features. By the end, readers will feel confident moving through the platform, finding essential tools, and understanding how the interface supports their tasks.

Overview of the SAP Concur Dashboard

The SAP Concur interface opens to the **Dashboard** or **Home Page**, where users see a personalized view of pending tasks, recent activity, and quick links to common functions. The dashboard is designed to be intuitive, allowing users to quickly access essential features and alerts, such as upcoming travel reservations, pending expense reports, and invoices awaiting approval.

1. **Task Pane**: On the main dashboard, a task pane often appears to the left, displaying tasks requiring attention, such as pending approvals,

incomplete travel bookings, or unsubmitted expense reports.

2. **Quick Links**: Centralized quick links provide fast access to frequently used functions like "Create New Expense Report" or "Book Travel."

3. **Alerts and Notifications**: Alerts notify users about policy violations, travel changes, or system updates, ensuring they stay informed of any immediate actions required.

Main Navigation Menu

The main navigation menu, usually found at the top of the screen, organizes SAP Concur's primary modules, including **Travel**, **Expense**, **Invoice**, **Reports**, and **Administration** (for users with administrator access).

- **Travel**: This tab allows users to book travel, view upcoming itineraries, and check travel policies.
- **Expense**: In the Expense section, users can create, submit, and manage expense reports, access recent transactions, and upload receipts.
- **Invoice**: The Invoice tab, typically for finance or accounts payable teams, provides access to manage vendor invoices, approve payments, and track spending by supplier.
- **Reports**: For data insights, this section contains reporting tools for generating expense, travel, and invoice summaries, enabling users to view spending trends and policy compliance.

- **Administration**: Only accessible to administrators, this tab includes tools for configuring the system, managing user roles, and adjusting policy settings.

Each of these tabs opens a secondary menu with additional options, providing users with a flexible and modular approach to navigating SAP Concur.

Navigating the Travel Module

The Travel module is designed to make booking travel simple and compliant with company policies. Here's a look at its core functions:

1. **Booking Travel**: The booking page includes fields to search for flights, hotels, rental cars, or trains. Users can specify travel dates, preferred times, and other details.
2. **My Trips**: This section displays a list of upcoming, current, and past trips. Each trip entry includes itinerary details, and users can modify or cancel bookings if needed.
3. **Travel Preferences**: The preferences page allows users to save travel preferences (e.g., preferred airlines or seating choices), simplifying future bookings.
4. **Travel Policies**: Displayed during booking, policy indicators show users whether a choice complies with company policies. SAP Concur flags non-

compliant options and may require additional approval if selected.

Navigating the Expense Module

The Expense module is a central tool for employees to report business expenses, submit receipts, and track reimbursements. Key areas include:

1. **Creating a New Expense Report**:
   - Users click **Create New Report** and input basic information, such as report name, purpose, and dates.
   - The report page allows users to add individual expenses, itemize transactions, and attach receipts.
2. **Adding Expenses**:
   - **Manual Entry**: Users can manually enter expense details, categorize expenses (e.g., meals, transportation), and input the amount.
   - **Corporate Card Transactions**: Corporate card transactions sync automatically, populating the user's expense list, where they can assign each charge to a report.
   - **Receipt Upload**: Users can upload receipts through the web interface or mobile app. SAP Concur uses Optical Character Recognition (OCR) to auto-fill data from receipts.

3. **Itemizing Expenses**:
   - Itemization breaks down expenses into specific categories, which is especially useful for hotel bills covering multiple categories like lodging, meals, and parking.
   - The itemization tool enables accurate categorization and compliance with reporting requirements.

4. **Submitting Reports**:
   - Once an expense report is complete, users can submit it for approval. SAP Concur routes it according to the pre-configured workflow, notifying managers or finance teams for review.
   - The submission page displays any policy violations, allowing users to correct or provide justifications as needed.

5. **Expense Report History**:
   - Users can review past expense reports, track statuses, and check for any rejected items needing revision. This feature allows employees to monitor reimbursements and address issues promptly.

Navigating the Invoice Module

The Invoice module is primarily used by finance teams to manage vendor invoices, approve payments, and track outstanding amounts. Here's an overview of the core functions:

1. **Invoice Capture**:
   - Invoices can be uploaded directly, either by scanning paper copies or importing digital versions.
   - SAP Concur's OCR tool extracts essential information, such as vendor name, amount, and invoice number, automating data entry.
2. **Invoice Approval Workflow**:
   - Each invoice follows a pre-set approval process based on its amount, type, or vendor. Users can view approval status, reassign approvers, or escalate invoices if necessary.
3. **Vendor Management**:
   - The vendor management tool provides a directory of all approved vendors, enabling finance teams to track spending by supplier and adjust payment terms as needed.
4. **Invoice Reporting**:
   - Like other modules, the Invoice module includes reporting tools to track total payments, overdue invoices, and spending trends by vendor.

Reporting Tools

SAP Concur's reporting tools provide valuable insights into company spending, helping management teams analyze expense patterns, identify savings opportunities, and ensure compliance. Here's how to access and use these tools:

1. **Standard Reports**:
   - Pre-configured reports cover areas like travel expenses, overdue invoices, and policy violations. Users can customize report parameters, such as date ranges and departments, to view specific data.
2. **Custom Reports**:
   - SAP Concur also allows users to create custom reports, choosing from a range of data fields and filters. For instance, a finance team could generate a report on travel expenses by region or analyze expenses by client project.
3. **Scheduled Reports**:
   - Reports can be scheduled to run automatically on a daily, weekly, or monthly basis, with results sent to selected users. This feature is ideal for managers who need regular expense updates without logging into SAP Concur.

4. **Exporting Reports**:
     ○ Reports can be exported in various
        formats, such as Excel or PDF, making it
        easy to share insights with other
        departments or include them in
        presentations.

Tips for Efficient Navigation

Navigating SAP Concur can be simplified with a few
helpful tips:

1. **Bookmarking Pages**:
     ○ Frequent users can bookmark essential
        pages within SAP Concur for quicker
        access, especially useful for managers
        who regularly approve expense reports
        or invoices.
2. **Utilizing the Mobile App**:
     ○ The SAP Concur mobile app offers a user-
        friendly interface for managing travel,
        expenses, and invoices on the go. It's
        especially useful for uploading receipts
        immediately after a transaction.
3. **Personalizing the Dashboard**:
     ○ Users can customize their dashboard
        layout, selecting which widgets appear,
        like pending tasks, recent activity, or
        policy alerts. A personalized dashboard
        can save time and enhance productivity.

4. **Using Search Functions**:
   - o The search bar, typically found at the top of each module, allows users to locate specific reports, invoices, or transactions quickly.

Common Issues and Troubleshooting

While SAP Concur's interface is designed to be intuitive, some users may encounter issues during navigation. Here are solutions to common problems:

1. **Error Messages During Submission**:
   - o If an error occurs when submitting an expense or invoice, check for policy violations or missing fields. SAP Concur often highlights specific errors to guide the user in resolving the issue.
2. **Missing Transactions or Receipts**:
   - o For missing corporate card transactions, users should verify that their card is correctly linked in their profile settings. For receipts, ensure they were uploaded and matched to the correct expense.
3. **Access Denied Errors**:
   - o Access errors often indicate a role-based restriction. If necessary, users can contact an SAP Concur administrator to adjust permissions or provide access to additional features.

Conclusion

This chapter has provided an in-depth tour of the SAP Concur interface, covering its primary modules—Travel, Expense, Invoice—and the reporting tools available. By familiarizing themselves with SAP Concur's navigation and tools, users can optimize their workflow, manage tasks efficiently, and take full advantage of the platform's capabilities.

In the following chapters, we'll dive deeper into each module, starting with the Travel module, where we'll explore travel booking, policy integration, and approval processes in detail.

This chapter gives thorough understanding of navigating SAP Concur, making it easier to perform their confidently.

Chapter 4: Configuring Travel Preferences

Introduction

Configuring travel preferences in SAP Concur enables organizations to control travel bookings, streamline employee travel experiences, and enforce compliance with company policies. Properly set travel preferences ensure that employees have access to preferred vendors, receive automatic travel policy enforcement, and enjoy a seamless booking process. In this chapter, we'll guide you through setting up travel preferences in SAP Concur, covering everything from choosing preferred vendors to configuring policy rules, and creating a streamlined travel booking experience for your organization.

Importance of Configuring Travel Preferences

Configuring travel preferences is essential for aligning travel bookings with company standards. The benefits of configuring these preferences include:

1. **Cost Control**: Setting travel preferences with pre-negotiated rates helps manage costs effectively, minimizing out-of-policy bookings and encouraging the use of approved vendors.
2. **Enhanced Compliance**: With automatic policy checks in place, SAP Concur helps enforce

corporate travel policies, reducing the risk of unauthorized bookings.

3. **Employee Satisfaction**: Employees benefit from streamlined booking options tailored to their needs, allowing them to book compliant travel quickly and easily.

4. **Improved Visibility**: Configuring travel preferences allows the organization to track travel activity and spending accurately, making it easier to analyze trends and manage budgets.

Step 1: Setting Up Preferred Vendors

The first step in configuring travel preferences is to identify and set up preferred vendors in SAP Concur. Preferred vendors are those with whom the company has special arrangements, such as discounted rates or exclusive benefits. Configuring these vendors ensures that employees have easy access to compliant options when booking travel.

1. **Identify Preferred Vendors**:
   - Collaborate with the procurement or finance team to identify preferred vendors for flights, hotels, car rentals, and ground transportation.
   - Ensure that these vendors align with company travel policies and offer benefits like discounted rates or additional amenities.

2. **Integrate Vendor Details**:
    - Within SAP Concur, add preferred vendors' details, including vendor names, preferred locations, and negotiated rates.
    - SAP Concur can often integrate directly with major travel providers, allowing employees to book services through the platform seamlessly.
3. **Vendor-Specific Policies**:
    - For each preferred vendor, set policies that define allowable rates, room types, or vehicle classes.
    - Establish policies for direct bookings with preferred vendors and ensure that preferred options are highlighted when employees make selections.

Step 2: Defining Travel Policy Rules

Defining travel policy rules in SAP Concur helps enforce compliance by automatically flagging out-of-policy bookings. Travel policies should reflect company standards, encourage cost-effective travel, and provide guidelines for appropriate bookings.

1. **Booking Classes and Travel Classes**:
    - Define booking classes for flights, hotels, and cars. For example, you may allow economy class for flights under five

hours, while business class could be permitted for longer journeys.

- o SAP Concur allows you to set automatic approval requirements for bookings outside defined classes.

2. **Setting Rate Limits**:
   - o Set maximum allowable rates for flights, hotels, and other travel options. For instance, you could set a maximum rate per night for hotel bookings, with options for city-based adjustments.
   - o SAP Concur flags bookings exceeding these rates, prompting users to choose compliant options or request special approval.

3. **Defining Pre-Approval Requirements**:
   - o Create pre-approval requirements for specific types of travel. For instance, require additional approval for international travel or bookings above a certain amount.
   - o Specify approvers within the policy, such as department heads or finance managers, to streamline the approval process.

4. **Establishing Booking Deadlines**:
   - o Encourage early booking by setting deadlines, such as requiring flights to be booked at least 14 days before departure.

- SAP Concur can notify employees if they try to book travel outside these timelines, helping to secure more cost-effective options.

Step 3: Configuring Traveler Profiles

Traveler profiles store individual travel preferences, making the booking experience more convenient for employees. Profiles can store preferences for seat selection, loyalty programs, and dietary needs.

1. **Profile Details**:
   - Employees can add personal details like contact information, passport numbers, and frequent flyer numbers.
   - Profile information is saved and used for all bookings, ensuring consistency and eliminating repetitive data entry.
2. **Preferred Seat and Meal Preferences**:
   - Travelers can specify seat preferences (e.g., aisle, window) and meal requirements (e.g., vegetarian, gluten-free) within their profiles.
   - SAP Concur applies these preferences automatically during bookings, creating a more personalized experience.
3. **Loyalty Programs and Memberships**:
   - Employees can add details for frequent flyer programs, hotel loyalty

memberships, and rental car
memberships.

- o SAP Concur will apply these loyalty
memberships to bookings when
applicable, allowing employees to earn
rewards while traveling for business.

Step 4: Setting Up Notifications and Alerts

Notifications and alerts in SAP Concur help employees
and managers stay informed about important travel-
related events, including upcoming travel, policy
violations, and booking changes.

1. **Booking Confirmation Alerts**:
   - o Set up booking confirmation alerts that
   notify employees when travel
   arrangements have been confirmed.
   These alerts can include itinerary details
   for easy reference.
2. **Policy Violation Notifications**:
   - o Configure alerts to notify employees if
   they select options that violate travel
   policies, such as out-of-policy hotel rates
   or non-preferred vendors.
   - o Managers can receive alerts for policy
   violations that require their approval,
   ensuring policy adherence while allowing
   flexibility when necessary.

3. **Travel Itinerary Reminders**:
   - Send reminders to travelers for upcoming trips, including departure times, check-in reminders, and travel document requirements.
   - These reminders can be particularly helpful for international travel, where employees may need additional documentation like visas.
4. **Emergency Alerts**:
   - For organizations with employees traveling in regions prone to disruptions, configure emergency alerts for timely notifications.
   - SAP Concur can send alerts related to flight cancellations, extreme weather, or political unrest, helping employees and managers make informed decisions.

Step 5: Configuring Approvals for Travel Bookings

Approval workflows for travel bookings ensure that travel plans align with organizational policies and budget constraints. SAP Concur allows you to define multi-level approval workflows, automatically routing requests to designated approvers.

1. **Defining Approval Hierarchies**:
   - Create approval hierarchies based on factors like employee role, department, and travel destination.
   - For instance, travel requests for high-level executives may require only basic approval, while international travel requests may require multiple levels of review.
2. **Configuring Conditional Approvals**:
   - Set conditional approvals based on trip details, such as bookings above a specified cost or international destinations.
   - SAP Concur can automatically forward these requests to senior management or finance for additional approval.
3. **Approval Notifications and Timelines**:
   - Send notifications to approvers as soon as a travel request is submitted, ensuring timely responses.
   - Set approval timelines to prevent delays, automatically escalating requests if no action is taken within a specified period.

Step 6: Integrating Travel Preferences with Expense Reporting

Integrating travel preferences with expense reporting provides a seamless experience, ensuring that travel expenses flow into expense reports automatically.

1. **Automatic Expense Import**:
   - Configure SAP Concur to automatically import travel expenses into expense reports, linking transactions to the appropriate categories.
   - This eliminates the need for manual data entry, saving employees time and reducing errors.
2. **Expense Policy Alignment**:
   - Align travel policies with expense policies, ensuring that expenses associated with travel bookings comply with the same standards.
   - For instance, if the travel policy limits meal expenses, the expense policy can automatically apply these limits to corresponding expenses.
3. **Reimbursement Tracking**:
   - Track reimbursement for travel-related expenses, such as meal allowances or mileage.
   - Employees can view reimbursable expenses linked to their travel itinerary,

providing clarity on eligible reimbursements.

Best Practices for Travel Preference Configuration

Configuring travel preferences effectively requires a strategic approach. Here are some best practices to follow:

1. **Keep Policies Flexible for Special Circumstances**:
   - While it's essential to enforce policies, consider exceptions for special circumstances, such as urgent travel needs or high-stress situations. Flexibility helps employees feel supported and can improve compliance.
2. **Encourage Employees to Complete Profiles**:
   - Encourage employees to complete their traveler profiles with accurate preferences and loyalty program information. A complete profile saves time during booking and reduces the likelihood of booking errors.
3. **Regularly Update Preferred Vendor Lists**:
   - Maintain a regular review process for preferred vendors to ensure they continue to offer competitive rates and services.
   - Update vendor lists as needed to provide employees with the best options and

ensure that preferred vendors align with current travel policies.

4. **Monitor Compliance and Adjust Policies**:
   o Use SAP Concur's reporting tools to monitor compliance with travel policies and identify areas where policies may need adjustment.
   o Regularly review compliance data to ensure that travel policies remain effective and support the organization's financial goals.

Conclusion

Configuring travel preferences in SAP Concur allows organizations to manage travel bookings effectively, enforcing compliance while streamlining the booking process for employees. By setting up preferred vendors, defining policy rules, configuring traveler profiles, and aligning approvals, organizations can create a cohesive travel management system that aligns with company standards. In the following chapter, we'll dive into creating and managing travel requests, offering a step-by-step guide to help employees book compliant travel with ease.

This chapter offers a thorough guide to configuring travel preferences in SAP Concur, helping understand the importance of policy compliance, vendor selection, and user customization in travel management.

Chapter 5: Creating and Managing Travel Requests

Introduction

Creating and managing travel requests in SAP Concur is an essential function for employees and managers alike. A travel request captures the details of a proposed business trip, ensuring compliance with company policies before booking begins. Managing travel requests efficiently helps streamline the approval process, minimize travel costs, and improve organizational transparency. This chapter will guide you through the steps of creating, submitting, and managing travel requests within SAP Concur, ensuring a seamless process for both employees and approvers.

Understanding the Purpose of Travel Requests

A travel request is a pre-trip authorization that allows employees to outline their planned travel, including expected costs, destinations, and duration. The purpose of travel requests is to:

1. **Ensure Policy Compliance**: Travel requests allow organizations to verify that planned travel aligns with company policies before costs are incurred.
2. **Gain Budgetary Approval**: Managers can assess the financial impact of a trip, granting approval only if the travel is justified and within budget.

3. **Streamline Bookings**: Approved travel requests automatically populate booking details, streamlining the process of arranging flights, hotels, and other travel accommodations.
4. **Enhance Visibility**: Travel requests give the organization a clear view of upcoming travel activities, making it easier to track spending and manage logistics.

Step-by-Step Guide to Creating a Travel Request

Creating a travel request in SAP Concur involves entering essential trip details, estimating expenses, and submitting the request for approval. Follow these steps to create a compliant travel request.

1. **Accessing the Travel Request Form**:
   - In the main navigation menu, click on the **Travel** tab, and select **Create New Request**.
   - This opens the travel request form, where employees can enter trip details and associated costs.
2. **Entering Basic Trip Information**:
   - **Trip Name**: Provide a descriptive name for the trip, such as "Client Meeting in San Francisco" or "Annual Sales Conference."

- **Travel Dates**: Specify the departure and return dates, including approximate times.
- **Destination**: Enter the primary location for the trip. SAP Concur may allow users to specify multiple locations if the trip involves different cities.
- **Purpose of Trip**: Select or enter the reason for travel, such as "Client Visit," "Training," or "Conference."

3. **Adding Expected Travel Costs**:
    - SAP Concur typically includes sections to estimate travel expenses, including transportation, lodging, meals, and miscellaneous costs.
    - **Transportation**: Enter the estimated cost for airfare, train tickets, or car rentals.
    - **Lodging**: Specify the number of nights and estimated nightly rate for hotel accommodations.
    - **Meals and Incidentals**: Estimate the daily allowance for meals and other incidental costs.
    - **Other Expenses**: Include any additional anticipated costs, such as visa fees or conference registration fees.

4. **Policy Compliance Check**:
    - SAP Concur checks the travel request against company policies, highlighting any out-of-policy items. For instance, a

high nightly hotel rate may trigger a policy flag.
- o Employees can adjust their request to align with policies or provide justifications for exceptions if necessary.

5. **Attaching Supporting Documents**:
   - o Employees can attach relevant documents to the travel request, such as an event invitation or client meeting agenda.
   - o Documents help approvers understand the purpose of the trip and verify the estimated costs.

6. **Submitting the Request for Approval**:
   - o Once all details are entered, click **Submit for Approval**. SAP Concur will route the request to the designated approver(s) based on the organization's approval hierarchy.
   - o The system notifies both the employee and approvers, confirming that the request is pending review.

Understanding the Approval Workflow for Travel Requests

SAP Concur's approval workflow is designed to ensure that travel requests undergo appropriate scrutiny before employees proceed with booking. Here's how the workflow typically operates:

1. **Automatic Routing to Approvers**:
   - Travel requests are automatically routed to approvers, usually based on the employee's role, department, or estimated trip cost.
   - For example, a department manager may review domestic travel requests, while higher-level executives handle international requests or those exceeding a certain budget.
2. **Multi-Level Approvals**:
   - For high-cost or international trips, SAP Concur can require multi-level approvals. This ensures that significant expenses are reviewed at multiple organizational levels.
   - Approvers receive notifications to review and either approve or reject the travel request.
3. **Conditional Approvals Based on Policy Compliance**:
   - Some requests may include conditional approvals, where requests with out-of-policy items are sent to higher-level approvers for review.
   - This flexibility allows for justified exceptions, ensuring that critical trips can proceed even if they fall outside standard policy limits.

4. **Tracking Approval Status:**
   - o Employees can monitor the status of their travel request, viewing details such as "Pending Approval," "Approved," or "Rejected."
   - o If additional information is needed, SAP Concur notifies the employee, allowing them to make necessary adjustments and resubmit.

Managing Approved Travel Requests

Once a travel request is approved, employees can proceed with bookings within SAP Concur. Approved requests serve as a blueprint for booking travel, ensuring that bookings match the planned itinerary.

1. **Converting Travel Requests to Bookings:**
   - o With approval in place, SAP Concur allows employees to create bookings directly from the travel request. This eliminates the need to re-enter details, as key information (e.g., dates, locations) transfers automatically.
   - o Employees can book flights, hotels, and transportation options while ensuring that all selections align with the approved request.

2. **Modifying Approved Requests**:
   - If travel plans change after approval, employees can modify their requests, adjusting dates, locations, or estimated costs as needed.
   - SAP Concur flags significant modifications, requiring re-approval from managers if changes impact the itinerary or budget substantially.
3. **Managing Cancellations**:
   - For trips that must be canceled, employees can withdraw their travel request. SAP Concur notifies relevant parties, canceling bookings and releasing funds or reservations.
   - This feature helps the organization avoid unnecessary costs and keeps records accurate.

Common Issues and Troubleshooting for Travel Requests

Travel requests may encounter issues such as policy violations or delayed approvals. Here's how to handle common challenges effectively:

1. **Policy Violation Flags**:
   - If SAP Concur flags a travel request for policy violations, review the flagged items and adjust the request as needed.

This may involve selecting different vendors, reducing costs, or adding justifications.

- o For justified exceptions, employees can add comments explaining the reason, which the approver can consider.

2. **Delayed Approvals:**
   - o If a travel request remains in "Pending Approval" status for an extended period, SAP Concur allows employees to send reminders to approvers.
   - o In cases of prolonged delays, employees can contact their manager or SAP Concur administrator to escalate the request.

3. **Errors in Estimated Costs:**
   - o If estimated costs in the request differ from actual booking prices, employees can modify the request or add comments to inform the approver of any expected differences.
   - o Maintaining clear and transparent communication regarding costs helps avoid issues during expense reimbursement.

Best Practices for Creating and Managing Travel Requests

Creating effective travel requests and managing them efficiently involves following best practices to ensure a smooth experience for all stakeholders.

1. **Provide Detailed Justifications for High-Cost Trips**:
   o   For expensive trips, add thorough justifications and supporting documents, such as conference agendas or client meeting schedules. This increases the likelihood of approval and helps approvers understand the value of the trip.
2. **Ensure Accuracy in Estimated Costs**:
   o   Provide accurate estimates for all aspects of the trip, including transportation, lodging, and meals. While some variations are expected, accurate estimates give approvers confidence in the budget.
3. **Review Policies Before Submitting Requests**:
   o   Familiarize yourself with company travel policies before submitting a request. This minimizes the chance of policy violations and improves approval times.

4. **Plan Travel Requests Well in Advance**:
   - Submit travel requests as early as possible to allow sufficient time for approvals. This also provides more options for cost-effective bookings, supporting company goals for budget-friendly travel.
5. **Use the Mobile App for Convenience**:
   - SAP Concur's mobile app allows employees to create and manage travel requests on the go. This is especially useful for last-minute trips or when employees need to adjust their requests quickly.

Leveraging Reports for Travel Requests

SAP Concur provides reporting tools that enable organizations to track travel requests and analyze travel spending patterns. Leveraging these reports can help managers optimize travel budgets and identify cost-saving opportunities.

1. **Travel Request Summary Reports**:
   - Summary reports provide an overview of all travel requests within a specified timeframe, helping managers see the volume and frequency of travel requests.

- o These reports can also indicate the average cost of trips, useful for budgeting purposes.
2. **Policy Compliance Reports**:
   - o Compliance reports show which travel requests include policy violations, highlighting areas where policy adjustments may be needed.
   - o By identifying frequent out-of-policy requests, the organization can modify travel policies to better align with employee needs or streamline compliance.
3. **Cost Analysis by Department**:
   - o SAP Concur allows managers to break down travel request data by department, showing travel frequency and costs at the departmental level.
   - o This data can inform decisions on department budgets and identify opportunities for cost reduction.

Conclusion

Creating and managing travel requests in SAP Concur is a straightforward yet crucial step in effective travel management. By following this chapter's guidelines, employees and managers can ensure that travel plans align with company policies, budgets, and approval processes. Travel requests help organizations maintain transparency, control costs, and simplify the booking process, providing a streamlined experience for all involved.

In the next chapter, we'll explore the booking process in detail, focusing on selecting compliant options, securing approvals, and managing travel itineraries.

This chapter provides a step-by-step guide to creating and managing travel requests, emphasizing the importance of policy compliance, budgeting, and approval workflows.

Chapter 6: Booking and Managing Trips

Introduction

Booking and managing trips in SAP Concur is a core function that allows employees to arrange travel efficiently while adhering to company policies. By integrating booking with pre-approved travel requests, SAP Concur ensures that each trip complies with organizational standards, enabling seamless management of flights, hotels, and ground transportation. This chapter will guide readers through the process of booking and managing trips, focusing on selecting compliant options, handling itineraries, and making adjustments as needed.

Overview of the Booking Process

In SAP Concur, booking a trip starts with an approved travel request. Once a request is approved, employees can use the system to arrange flights, accommodations, and transportation within the parameters of the approval. SAP Concur's booking tools allow employees to:

1. **Access Preferred Vendors and Rates**: SAP Concur highlights preferred vendors with pre-negotiated rates, helping employees select cost-effective and compliant options.

2. **Ensure Policy Compliance**: The platform checks booking selections against company policies, alerting users to any out-of-policy choices.
3. **Manage Itineraries in Real-Time**: Employees can view, modify, or cancel their bookings as needed, with automatic updates sent to their itineraries.

Step 1: Starting the Booking Process

Once a travel request has been approved, employees can proceed to book their travel within SAP Concur. Here's a step-by-step guide to initiating the booking process.

1. **Accessing the Approved Request**:
   - Navigate to the **Travel** tab in the SAP Concur dashboard and locate the approved travel request.
   - Click on **Book Travel** to begin the booking process, automatically pulling in the trip details from the approved request.
2. **Choosing the Travel Type**:
   - SAP Concur typically presents options for booking flights, hotels, and rental cars. Users can select one or multiple travel types as needed for their trip.
   - For example, if the employee is only booking a flight and hotel, they can skip the car rental option and proceed

directly to hotel booking after selecting a
flight.

Step 2: Booking Flights

SAP Concur's flight booking interface is designed to
simplify the selection of compliant, cost-effective flights.
Here's how to book flights efficiently:

1. **Entering Flight Details**:
    - Enter the departure and arrival cities,
      dates, and times based on the approved
      travel request. SAP Concur displays a list
      of flights meeting these criteria.
    - Employees can filter results by airline,
      departure time, or price, making it easy
      to find the best option.
2. **Identifying Preferred Options**:
    - SAP Concur highlights flights with
      preferred airlines and within policy-
      compliant fare ranges, often indicated by
      a "preferred" label or icon.
    - Selecting a preferred option ensures
      compliance with company policies and
      helps employees avoid out-of-policy
      selections.
3. **Viewing Policy Compliance Flags**:
    - If an employee selects an out-of-policy
      flight, SAP Concur flags the choice and
      may require a justification or additional

approval. For instance, selecting a premium economy seat when only economy is approved will prompt a policy violation notification.

- o Employees can either adjust their selection to a compliant option or submit a justification if the out-of-policy selection is necessary.

4. **Booking the Flight**:
   - o Once a compliant flight is chosen, click **Select** to view the flight's details, including fare breakdown and cancellation policies.
   - o Click **Book** to finalize the flight selection. SAP Concur automatically adds the flight to the employee's itinerary and sends a booking confirmation.

Step 3: Booking Accommodations

After securing a flight, employees can proceed to book accommodations, such as hotels or other lodging, in line with company travel policies.

1. **Searching for Hotels**:
   - o Enter the destination city, check-in and check-out dates, and any preferred criteria, such as proximity to a meeting location or airport.

      o   SAP Concur displays a list of available hotels, highlighting preferred options or those within the approved nightly rate.

2. **Applying Filters for Convenience**:
   - Employees can filter hotel options by amenities (e.g., Wi-Fi, breakfast), star rating, or distance from the specified location.
   - This feature ensures employees can select accommodations that meet both their needs and company policies.

3. **Evaluating Policy Compliance**:
   - SAP Concur flags hotels outside the company's approved rate range or those without required amenities, such as internet access for business purposes.
   - Employees are encouraged to select a compliant hotel, but can provide justifications if a non-compliant option is chosen (e.g., proximity to an important meeting).

4. **Completing the Booking**:
   - Once a hotel is selected, click **Book** to finalize the reservation. SAP Concur adds the hotel booking to the itinerary and sends a confirmation to the employee's email.

Step 4: Booking Ground Transportation

For many trips, ground transportation, such as rental cars or ride-sharing, is essential. SAP Concur simplifies the process of booking ground transportation in a compliant manner.

1. **Rental Car Bookings**:
   - If a rental car is required, SAP Concur presents options for booking based on the travel request.
   - Employees can specify pick-up and drop-off locations, dates, and times. The platform displays options from preferred car rental vendors, helping employees select compliant rental choices.
2. **Ground Transportation Policies**:
   - Many organizations limit rental car bookings to specific vehicle classes (e.g., compact or standard). SAP Concur enforces these limits, ensuring employees select policy-compliant vehicles.
   - If the employee chooses a vehicle outside of approved classes, SAP Concur flags the selection and may require additional approval.
3. **Alternative Ground Transportation**:
   - For trips where a rental car is not necessary, employees may choose ride-

sharing or taxi services. While these options aren't booked directly within SAP Concur, they can be included in expense reports after the trip.

4. **Finalizing Ground Transportation**:
   - Once a compliant rental option is chosen, click **Book** to add the ground transportation to the itinerary. SAP Concur sends a confirmation email, including rental details.

Step 5: Reviewing and Managing the Itinerary

Once all travel components are booked, SAP Concur consolidates them into a single itinerary, allowing employees to view and manage all travel details in one place.

1. **Accessing the Itinerary**:
   - The complete itinerary, including flight, hotel, and car rental details, is available on the **Travel** tab under **My Trips**.
   - The itinerary includes all booking confirmations, contact details for airlines, hotels, and rental car agencies, and policy compliance information.

2. **Making Changes to the Itinerary**:
   - SAP Concur allows employees to modify or cancel bookings directly from their itinerary. For example, they can change a

flight time or extend a hotel stay if needed.

- o Some changes may require re-approval if they affect trip costs or policy compliance.

3. **Receiving Itinerary Updates**:
   - o Employees receive real-time notifications for any changes to their itinerary, such as flight delays or gate changes.
   - o These updates help employees stay informed and make necessary adjustments during travel.

Handling Cancellations and Modifications

Unexpected changes are common in business travel, and SAP Concur provides tools for managing cancellations or modifications efficiently.

1. **Canceling a Trip**:
   - o To cancel an entire trip, go to the **My Trips** section, select the trip, and choose **Cancel**.
   - o SAP Concur cancels all booked components (flights, hotels, rentals) and sends a notification to relevant parties, such as managers and finance teams.

2. **Modifying a Booking**:
   - o For changes to specific bookings (e.g., flight rescheduling), employees can

modify individual components through the itinerary.
- o Some modifications, such as selecting a new flight time, may trigger a policy compliance check, requiring employees to select compliant options or justify the changes.

3. **Refunds and Credits**:
   - o Canceled bookings may result in refunds or travel credits. SAP Concur records these, allowing employees to apply credits to future bookings when available.
   - o Finance teams can track these credits, ensuring efficient use of funds and managing the organization's travel budget effectively.

Best Practices for Booking and Managing Trips

Effectively booking and managing trips requires attention to policy compliance, efficient use of resources, and proactive communication. Here are some best practices to follow:

1. **Book as Early as Possible**:
   - o Early booking allows employees to secure preferred vendors and comply with booking deadlines, often leading to cost savings and better options.

2. **Stay Within Policy Limits**:
   - o Employees should always prioritize in-policy options and only request exceptions when absolutely necessary. Complying with policy limits streamlines the approval process and keeps travel costs manageable.

3. **Use the Mobile App for On-the-Go Management**:
   - o SAP Concur's mobile app is ideal for managing bookings on the go, including receiving real-time updates, adjusting itineraries, and accessing confirmations quickly.

4. **Monitor Itinerary Updates Closely**:
   - o Staying updated on itinerary changes helps employees respond promptly to travel disruptions, like flight delays or cancellations, minimizing travel stress.

5. **Communicate Changes Promptly**:
   - o For significant changes to the itinerary, such as rescheduling a return flight, employees should inform their manager to ensure alignment with business needs and budget.

Conclusion

Booking and managing trips in SAP Concur is a streamlined process designed to balance policy compliance with employee convenience. By following the guidelines in this chapter, employees can secure travel arrangements that meet organizational standards while enjoying a simplified booking experience.

In the next chapter, we will cover **Integrating Corporate Travel Policies**.

This chapter provides a comprehensive guide to booking and managing trips, emphasizing the importance of policy adherence, effective itinerary management, and proactive communication.

Chapter 7: Integrating Corporate Travel Policies

Introduction

Integrating corporate travel policies in SAP Concur is essential for managing travel expenses, ensuring compliance, and providing a clear framework for employees booking travel. Well-defined travel policies support cost control, minimize compliance risks, and provide consistent guidelines that employees can follow. This chapter explores how to establish, configure, and enforce travel policies within SAP Concur, guiding you through the steps to integrate corporate travel policies effectively.

The Importance of Travel Policies in Corporate Travel Management

Corporate travel policies define the rules for booking travel, covering areas such as preferred vendors, allowable rates, and reimbursement limits. Integrating these policies into SAP Concur offers several benefits:

1. **Cost Management**: Policies control expenses by setting limits on allowable costs for flights, accommodations, and meals, helping organizations stay within budget.
2. **Enhanced Compliance**: Policy enforcement in SAP Concur helps employees follow established

guidelines, reducing the risk of unauthorized expenses.

3. **Improved Efficiency**: Automated policy checks in SAP Concur streamline the booking and approval process, minimizing back-and-forth and reducing the burden on managers.

4. **Consistency Across the Organization**: Integrated travel policies provide a standardized framework for all employees, ensuring consistent practices regardless of department or location.

Step 1: Defining Corporate Travel Policy Requirements

Before configuring travel policies in SAP Concur, it's essential to define the scope and objectives of your corporate travel policies. This includes specifying allowable expenses, identifying preferred vendors, and establishing limits on travel classes and accommodations.

1. **Determine Expense Categories and Limits**:
   - Identify the categories covered by the policy, such as flights, lodging, meals, ground transportation, and incidentals.
   - Set spending limits for each category based on location or travel purpose. For instance, the policy might specify a daily meal allowance for domestic versus international travel.

2. **Identify Preferred Vendors**:
   - Preferred vendors are airlines, hotels, and rental car agencies with whom the organization has negotiated favorable rates.
   - Specify preferred vendors in the policy to encourage employees to book with these partners, supporting cost control and consistency.

3. **Define Travel Class Restrictions**:
   - Define the class of travel allowed for different types of trips. For example, the policy may limit economy class for domestic flights but allow business class for international flights exceeding a specific duration.

4. **Specify Approval Requirements**:
   - Outline any pre-approval requirements for certain types of trips, such as high-cost travel or travel to specific regions.
   - Indicate the level of approval required based on employee role or estimated trip cost, which will later inform SAP Concur's automated approval workflow.

5. **Set Policy Exceptions**:
   - Identify exceptions to standard policy rules for special circumstances, such as emergency travel, long-duration trips, or travel to high-cost regions.

- Policies should clearly outline the process for requesting exceptions and the conditions under which they may be granted.

Step 2: Configuring Policy Settings in SAP Concur

Once corporate travel policies are defined, configure them in SAP Concur. The platform's policy settings allow for detailed customization, enabling organizations to enforce their unique travel standards effectively.

1. **Accessing Policy Configuration in SAP Concur**:
   - Go to the **Administration** or **Policy Settings** tab in SAP Concur, depending on user permissions.
   - Select **Travel Policy Settings** to access the configuration options for travel-related expenses, bookings, and vendor preferences.
2. **Configuring Policy Limits by Category**:
   - Set spending limits for each category, including flights, hotels, meals, and incidentals. SAP Concur allows for location-based limits, which can vary by region or travel type.
   - For example, set a maximum nightly rate for hotel accommodations or a per-diem limit for meals.

3. **Setting Up Preferred Vendors**:
   - Under the **Vendor Preferences** section, specify preferred airlines, hotels, and rental agencies.
   - Assign preferred status to these vendors to make them visible during bookings. SAP Concur highlights preferred options, encouraging employees to book with these vendors.

4. **Enforcing Travel Class and Fare Restrictions**:
   - Configure restrictions on travel classes, such as limiting domestic flights to economy class. SAP Concur applies these restrictions automatically, flagging any non-compliant selections.
   - For fare restrictions, set limits on maximum allowable fare levels, helping employees avoid high-cost options.

5. **Defining Approval Rules**:
   - In the **Approval Settings** section, set rules for different approval levels based on factors such as trip cost, destination, and employee role.
   - Configure conditional approval requirements, such as additional approval for international travel or bookings outside the allowable fare range.

6. **Creating Policy Exceptions**:
   - Add exceptions for specific circumstances, allowing SAP Concur to accommodate unique travel needs while maintaining compliance.
   - For example, you can create an exception for business-class flights on trips exceeding eight hours or hotel rates in high-cost areas.

Step 3: Enabling Automated Policy Checks

SAP Concur's automated policy checks help enforce travel policies by flagging out-of-policy selections in real time. These checks prompt employees to make compliant choices, reducing the need for manual intervention.

1. **Enabling Real-Time Policy Notifications**:
   - Configure SAP Concur to display notifications during the booking process if a selection violates the travel policy.
   - For example, if an employee selects a hotel that exceeds the nightly rate limit, SAP Concur displays a notification, allowing the employee to choose a compliant option.
2. **Flagging Non-Compliant Bookings**:
   - SAP Concur flags non-compliant bookings, indicating any areas that

exceed policy limits or use non-preferred vendors.
- o Employees can adjust their choices to meet policy requirements or submit a justification if a policy exception is necessary.

3. **Sending Automatic Approval Requests**:
   - o For non-compliant selections requiring approval, SAP Concur routes the booking to the appropriate approver automatically.
   - o Approvers receive an email or app notification, allowing them to review the non-compliant booking, approve the exception, or request changes.

Step 4: Communicating Travel Policies to Employees

Effective policy integration requires employees to understand the travel policies, their purpose, and how SAP Concur enforces them. Clear communication reduces confusion and increases policy compliance.

1. **Distribute Policy Documents**:
   - o Make the travel policy accessible to all employees, either through the company's intranet, HR portal, or SAP Concur itself.
   - o Ensure that employees know where to find the latest version of the policy and

that they are aware of any updates or changes.

2. **Provide Training on SAP Concur Policy Enforcement**:
   - Offer training on how SAP Concur enforces travel policies, highlighting features like automated notifications, preferred vendor selection, and policy flags.
   - Employees should understand the policy compliance process, including how to respond to flagged items or request exceptions.

3. **Encourage Use of Preferred Vendors**:
   - Emphasize the importance of booking with preferred vendors and explain the benefits, such as discounted rates or added amenities.
   - Regular reminders about preferred vendors can reinforce compliance and help employees make informed booking choices.

4. **Explain the Exception Process**:
   - Clearly outline the process for requesting exceptions to standard travel policies, specifying when and how employees can submit justifications.
   - This helps employees understand that while policies are essential, the company

accommodates special circumstances when justified.

Monitoring Policy Compliance and Making Adjustments

SAP Concur's reporting tools enable organizations to monitor policy compliance and identify trends in employee travel behavior. By analyzing this data, organizations can make informed adjustments to their travel policies.

1. **Generating Compliance Reports**:
    o Use SAP Concur's reporting module to create compliance reports that highlight instances of policy violations, common exceptions, and adherence to preferred vendor guidelines.
    o Compliance reports provide visibility into how well employees follow policies and whether adjustments are needed.
2. **Analyzing Travel Spending Trends**:
    o Examine trends in travel spending, such as average expenses per trip or most frequently used vendors. These insights help organizations identify areas where policies may need tightening or relaxing.
    o For instance, if hotel rates frequently exceed policy limits in a particular city,

adjusting the allowable rate for that region can improve compliance.

3. **Adjusting Policies Based on Data Insights**:
   - Based on compliance data, make data-driven adjustments to policies. For example, if employees frequently need higher daily meal allowances for international travel, adjusting the per-diem rate can help align policy with actual needs.
   - Regular policy reviews ensure that guidelines remain relevant and support both cost control and employee satisfaction.

4. **Providing Feedback to Employees**:
   - Share insights from compliance monitoring with employees, highlighting areas of strong compliance and areas for improvement.
   - Positive reinforcement for compliant travel behavior can encourage continued adherence to travel policies.

Best Practices for Integrating Corporate Travel Policies

To ensure that travel policy integration in SAP Concur is effective, follow these best practices:

1. **Keep Policies Clear and Flexible**:
   o Use clear, concise language in travel policies, avoiding ambiguous terms. Flexibility for special cases or high-cost regions can increase employee satisfaction and reduce compliance issues.
2. **Regularly Update Travel Policies**:
   o Review and update policies at least annually to ensure they reflect current market rates, vendor relationships, and organizational needs.
3. **Involve Key Stakeholders in Policy Design**:
   o Engage departments like finance, HR, and department heads when creating or updating travel policies to ensure the guidelines support organizational goals across all levels.
4. **Encourage Feedback from Employees**:
   o Encourage employees to share their experiences and challenges with travel policies, particularly regarding compliance issues. This feedback can help refine policies and improve employee compliance.

Conclusion

Integrating corporate travel policies in SAP Concur ensures that travel arrangements align with organizational goals for cost control, compliance, and efficiency. By following this chapter's guidelines, organizations can establish, enforce, and monitor travel policies effectively, supporting both employee satisfaction and financial discipline.

In the next chapter, we will explore reporting and analytics in SAP Concur, diving into how data insights can drive strategic decisions and optimize travel management.

This chapter provides a comprehensive guide to integrating and managing travel policies within SAP Concur, emphasizing policy configuration, enforcement, and monitoring.

Complete Guide to Travel, Expense, and Invoice Management.

Chapter 8: Travel Reporting and Analytics

Introduction

Travel reporting and analytics in SAP Concur enable organizations to gain valuable insights into travel spending, policy compliance, and overall travel efficiency. By leveraging data, organizations can make data-driven decisions, optimize travel policies, and identify cost-saving opportunities. This chapter will explore how to use SAP Concur's reporting and analytics tools, focusing on the different types of reports available, creating custom reports, interpreting data, and using insights to refine travel management strategies.

The Importance of Travel Reporting and Analytics

Effective reporting and analytics are crucial for managing corporate travel. Travel data allows organizations to:

1. **Control Costs**: Reporting tools provide insights into travel spending, helping organizations identify areas for cost savings and budget control.
2. **Improve Compliance**: Analytics help monitor compliance with travel policies, identifying

trends in policy violations and informing necessary adjustments.

3. **Enhance Decision-Making**: Data-driven insights enable more informed decisions, from vendor partnerships to policy changes.
4. **Optimize Travel Policies**: Analyzing travel patterns and expenses helps refine policies to better align with organizational needs and employee behaviors.

Overview of Reporting Tools in SAP Concur

SAP Concur's reporting tools offer a range of standard and custom reports designed to cover all aspects of travel management. Some key features include:

- **Standard Reports**: Pre-built reports covering common travel metrics such as spending, compliance, and vendor usage.
- **Custom Reports**: The ability to create reports tailored to specific needs, selecting from various data fields and filters.
- **Scheduled Reports**: Automated reporting options that generate reports on a recurring basis, such as weekly or monthly.
- **Exporting Data**: Reports can be exported in multiple formats (e.g., PDF, Excel) for further analysis or sharing with stakeholders.

Key Types of Standard Travel Reports

SAP Concur offers a variety of standard reports that provide insights into travel spending, policy compliance, vendor usage, and more. These reports cover common reporting needs and can be accessed easily within the system.

1. **Travel Spend Analysis**:
   - This report provides a breakdown of travel expenses by category, such as flights, lodging, and ground transportation. It allows organizations to analyze travel spending trends and identify high-cost areas.
   - Spending data can be filtered by department, employee, or time period, making it easy to see where budgets are being allocated.
2. **Policy Compliance Report**:
   - The Policy Compliance report shows the frequency and type of policy violations, helping organizations understand how well employees are following travel policies.
   - It highlights common non-compliance issues, such as out-of-policy bookings, allowing management to adjust policies or address specific behaviors.

3. **Vendor Utilization Report**:
   - This report tracks usage of preferred vendors (e.g., airlines, hotels, car rental agencies), helping organizations assess the effectiveness of vendor partnerships.
   - By analyzing vendor utilization, companies can negotiate better rates with frequently used vendors and ensure that employees are booking with approved partners.
4. **Top Travelers Report**:
   - The Top Travelers report identifies employees who travel most frequently or incur the highest travel expenses. This data can be useful for travel managers who need to monitor high-volume travelers.
   - Top traveler data can inform decisions on travel benefits, loyalty programs, or policy adjustments for frequent travelers.
5. **Trip Details Report**:
   - This report provides a detailed view of each trip, including itinerary, cost, and booking details. It's particularly useful for tracking trip-specific costs and ensuring alignment with approved travel requests.
   - Trip details can be used to review individual travel experiences, track travel patterns, and support trip audits.

Creating Custom Reports in SAP Concur

In addition to standard reports, SAP Concur allows users to create custom reports tailored to their specific needs. Custom reports provide flexibility in selecting data fields, filters, and display formats, enabling more detailed analysis.

1. **Accessing the Custom Report Builder**:
   - In SAP Concur's **Reports** section, select **Create Custom Report** to access the report-building tool.
   - The tool allows users to select data categories (e.g., spending, policy compliance, traveler details) and customize fields for the report.
2. **Selecting Data Fields**:
   - Choose relevant data fields based on the report's purpose. For instance, a report on travel costs may include fields like travel category, amount, and vendor.
   - SAP Concur provides a wide range of fields, from trip details and employee information to policy compliance and approval status.
3. **Applying Filters**:
   - Use filters to refine the data displayed in the report. For example, filter by date range, department, destination, or travel type.

- Filtering options allow organizations to focus on specific areas, such as a department's quarterly travel expenses or international trips only.

4. **Configuring Report Layout**:
   - Configure the report's layout, choosing between table or chart formats based on the data's presentation needs.
   - Users can set groupings (e.g., by department or travel category) and sort data to highlight key insights.

5. **Saving and Running the Report**:
   - Once the custom report is configured, save the report for future use. SAP Concur allows users to save multiple custom reports for quick access.
   - Click **Run Report** to generate the data. The report can then be reviewed, edited, or exported for further analysis.

Scheduling and Automating Reports

For ongoing reporting needs, SAP Concur offers scheduling options that allow users to set up automated, recurring reports. This feature saves time and ensures that stakeholders receive updated travel data regularly.

1. **Setting a Report Schedule**:
   - In the report settings, select **Schedule Report** and specify the frequency (e.g., daily, weekly, monthly).
   - Choose a start date and set the time for report generation, ensuring it aligns with the needs of the recipients.
2. **Selecting Recipients**:
   - Add recipients to receive the scheduled reports, such as department heads, finance team members, or travel managers.
   - Scheduled reports can be shared internally and help keep relevant teams informed on travel spending and policy compliance.
3. **Monitoring Scheduled Reports**:
   - SAP Concur provides a list of scheduled reports, allowing users to monitor active reports and make adjustments as needed.
   - Users can edit report criteria, update recipients, or adjust the schedule to meet changing reporting requirements.

Interpreting Travel Data for Insights

Interpreting travel data is crucial for extracting actionable insights. Understanding the data in SAP Concur's reports can help organizations optimize travel policies, negotiate with vendors, and identify cost-saving opportunities.

1. **Analyzing Spending Trends**:
   - Review the **Travel Spend Analysis** report to identify high-cost areas, such as frequent use of premium flights or expensive hotels.
   - Look for spending patterns over time, such as seasonal variations in travel costs, to improve budget planning and control.
2. **Identifying Non-Compliance Trends**:
   - Use the **Policy Compliance Report** to detect recurring policy violations. For example, if many employees are booking out-of-policy hotels, consider updating the policy to meet employee needs or reinforcing existing guidelines.
   - Track non-compliance rates by department or travel type to identify specific areas requiring intervention.
3. **Evaluating Vendor Performance**:
   - The **Vendor Utilization Report** helps assess preferred vendors' performance. Low utilization rates for preferred vendors may indicate a need to re-evaluate vendor contracts or educate employees on preferred options.

- High utilization of certain vendors can support negotiating better rates, improving cost efficiency.
4. **Optimizing Travel Policies**:
   - Based on compliance data and spending trends, refine travel policies to reflect real-world needs. For example, adjust hotel rate limits for high-cost cities or increase meal allowances for international trips.
   - Data-driven policy adjustments help improve employee satisfaction and streamline compliance.

Exporting and Sharing Reports

SAP Concur's export options allow users to share reports with key stakeholders for collaborative analysis. Exported reports can also be incorporated into presentations, financial reviews, and strategic planning sessions.

1. **Exporting Reports**:
   - Select **Export** in the report settings to choose the format, such as PDF, Excel, or CSV. Excel and CSV formats are useful for further data manipulation and analysis.
   - Exported reports retain all formatting and data, ensuring that the report's integrity is maintained during sharing.

2. **Incorporating Reports in Presentations**:
    - o Use reports in executive presentations to highlight travel performance, policy compliance, and spending trends.
    - o Visual data, such as charts and graphs from SAP Concur reports, can help stakeholders understand key insights quickly.
3. **Sharing Insights with Departments**:
    - o Share relevant data with departments or teams, particularly if the report highlights department-specific trends or improvement areas.
    - o Regular reporting keeps departments accountable for their travel spending and compliance with policies.

Best Practices for Travel Reporting and Analytics

To maximize the benefits of SAP Concur's reporting tools, follow these best practices:

1. **Schedule Regular Review Sessions**:
    - o Review travel data regularly, such as quarterly or biannually, to monitor trends and make timely policy adjustments. Regular reviews allow organizations to respond to changing travel patterns effectively.

2. **Involve Stakeholders in Analysis**:
   o Engage finance, HR, and department managers in reviewing travel reports. Their input can provide additional context, supporting more accurate insights and data-driven decisions.
3. **Set Goals for Cost and Compliance**:
   o Establish specific goals for travel cost reduction or compliance improvement. For instance, set a goal to reduce out-of-policy bookings by a certain percentage each quarter.
   o Use SAP Concur's reporting data to track progress toward these goals and make adjustments as needed.
4. **Leverage Benchmarking**:
   o Benchmark travel spending and compliance rates against industry standards or internal metrics. Benchmarking provides a point of reference for measuring the effectiveness of travel policies.
5. **Create a Data-Driven Feedback Loop**:
   o Use insights from reporting to continuously improve travel policies, employee education, and vendor relationships. A feedback loop helps refine travel management practices over time, leading to sustained improvements.

Conclusion

SAP Concur's reporting and analytics tools empower organizations to manage travel more effectively, using data insights to control costs, enhance compliance, and improve decision-making. By utilizing standard reports, creating custom analyses, and interpreting travel data thoughtfully, organizations can develop strategies that optimize travel management and support long-term goals.

In the next chapter, we will explore **Configuring Expense Policies**.

This chapter provides a comprehensive guide to SAP Concur's reporting and analytics features, enabling organizations to gain meaningful insights from travel data.

Chapter 9: Configuring Expense Policies

Introduction

Configuring expense policies in SAP Concur is essential for managing corporate expenses, ensuring compliance, and controlling costs. By setting up clear guidelines for allowable expenses, spending limits, and approval workflows, organizations can create a seamless and compliant expense reporting process. This chapter will guide you through the steps of configuring expense policies in SAP Concur, covering policy creation, limits, automated compliance checks, and best practices for maintaining effective expense management.

Importance of Configuring Expense Policies

Expense policies provide a structured approach to expense management, ensuring that all employee expenses align with organizational standards. Key benefits of configuring expense policies in SAP Concur include:

1. **Enhanced Compliance**: Policies enforce spending rules, helping employees understand what is allowable and minimizing unauthorized expenses.

2. **Cost Control**: By setting limits on various expense categories, organizations can better manage budgets and avoid excessive spending.
3. **Streamlined Approvals**: Clear policies simplify the approval process, allowing managers to make quick, consistent decisions.
4. **Reduced Risk of Fraud**: Automated checks in SAP Concur flag potential policy violations, reducing the risk of fraudulent or inflated expenses.

Step 1: Defining Expense Policy Components

Before configuring expense policies in SAP Concur, it's important to define the components of your policy. Each component establishes rules and guidelines for specific types of expenses and spending limits.

1. **Identify Expense Categories**:
   - Define categories for common expenses, such as meals, lodging, transportation, mileage, office supplies, and entertainment.
   - Consider creating sub-categories if needed, such as "Domestic Lodging" versus "International Lodging," to address specific policy requirements.
2. **Set Spending Limits**:
   - Establish maximum allowable amounts for each expense category. For instance,

you may set a per-diem rate for meals and a nightly limit for hotel stays.
- o Spending limits can vary by location, travel type (domestic vs. international), or employee role to accommodate different travel costs and needs.

3. **Define Receipt Requirements**:
   - o Determine when receipts are required for expense submissions. Commonly, receipts are required for expenses above a specific threshold, such as $25 or $50.
   - o Clearly outline the required information on receipts, such as vendor name, date, and amount, to avoid incomplete submissions.

4. **Set Reimbursement Guidelines**:
   - o Define reimbursement rules, including allowable expenses, limits, and timelines for submission. These rules help employees understand what qualifies for reimbursement and when to submit claims.

5. **Outline Approval Requirements**:
   - o Specify which expenses require manager approval, and if necessary, establish a multi-level approval process for high-cost expenses.
   - o Approval requirements may vary based on factors like expense amount, employee role, or policy exceptions.

6. **Establish Policy Exceptions**:
    - ○ Define exceptions to standard policies for unique circumstances, such as emergency travel, business meetings with clients, or high-cost regions.
    - ○ Clearly communicate the process for requesting exceptions to ensure employees know when and how exceptions apply.

Step 2: Configuring Expense Categories in SAP Concur

With the components of your expense policy defined, you can begin configuring them in SAP Concur. Expense categories form the backbone of your policy configuration, organizing expenses for tracking, reporting, and compliance.

1. **Access the Expense Policy Settings**:
    - ○ In SAP Concur, navigate to the **Administration** or **Policy Settings** section, and select **Expense Policy** to access configuration options.
    - ○ Choose **Expense Categories** to define categories and sub-categories that align with your organization's needs.
2. **Setting Up Expense Categories and Limits**:
    - ○ For each category, set a spending limit that reflects the policy. For example,

define a daily allowance for meals or a per-mile reimbursement for mileage.

- SAP Concur allows users to set different limits based on location, travel type, or employee role, ensuring flexibility in policy enforcement.

3. **Configuring Expense Categories by Location**:
   - Create location-specific categories for expenses like lodging and meals. For instance, establish separate lodging limits for high-cost cities and international destinations.
   - SAP Concur's location-based settings make it easy to account for regional cost differences, improving compliance without overburdening employees.

4. **Enabling Required Fields for Submissions**:
   - For each expense category, specify required fields to ensure complete submissions. For example, set required fields for "vendor name," "date," and "purpose" for entertainment expenses.
   - SAP Concur flags incomplete expense entries, reducing the risk of missing information and ensuring compliance with submission standards.

Step 3: Configuring Receipt Requirements

Receipt requirements are an essential part of expense policies, ensuring accurate reporting and preventing errors. Configuring these requirements in SAP Concur helps employees understand when receipts are necessary and what information they should contain.

1. **Setting Receipt Thresholds**:
   - Define receipt thresholds based on expense amount. For example, require receipts for expenses over $25, while smaller expenses may not require documentation.
   - SAP Concur allows you to configure receipt requirements by category, providing flexibility in the level of documentation required.
2. **Enabling OCR (Optical Character Recognition)**:
   - Enable OCR for receipt uploads in SAP Concur, allowing the system to extract data automatically. OCR technology reads receipt information and populates fields like vendor name, amount, and date.
   - OCR reduces manual entry and helps employees submit accurate expense details with ease.

3. **Flagging Missing Receipts**:
   - o Configure SAP Concur to flag missing receipts automatically, notifying employees of incomplete submissions.
   - o Employees can add missing receipts to flagged items, ensuring that each expense entry meets documentation requirements.

Step 4: Configuring Automated Compliance Checks

Automated compliance checks in SAP Concur streamline expense policy enforcement, flagging policy violations and guiding employees toward compliant choices. These checks improve efficiency by reducing manual oversight and maintaining consistent policy enforcement.

1. **Enabling Real-Time Compliance Notifications**:
   - o Configure SAP Concur to notify employees in real-time if they attempt to submit out-of-policy expenses. Notifications appear during expense entry, prompting employees to adjust their entries as needed.
   - o Real-time notifications reduce the likelihood of policy violations, making it easier for employees to correct issues before submission.

2. **Setting Up Compliance Flags**:
   - For each category, configure compliance flags for policy violations, such as exceeding spending limits, selecting non-preferred vendors, or failing to attach receipts.
   - Compliance flags alert employees and approvers, allowing them to address issues promptly and ensuring compliance with expense policies.

3. **Defining Conditional Approvals**:
   - Configure conditional approvals for out-of-policy expenses, such as expenses above a certain threshold. SAP Concur routes these submissions to designated approvers for additional review.
   - Conditional approvals allow flexibility in policy enforcement while ensuring that high-cost or unusual expenses receive appropriate oversight.

4. **Automating Expense Report Submission Checks**:
   - Set up automatic checks to ensure that expense reports meet all submission criteria, including receipt requirements, policy compliance, and documentation.
   - SAP Concur flags incomplete reports, prompting employees to make necessary adjustments before submitting their expenses for approval.

Step 5: Defining Approval Workflows for Expense Policies

Approval workflows provide structure to the expense approval process, ensuring that all expenses align with organizational policies and receive appropriate review. In SAP Concur, you can define multi-level approval workflows based on expense type, amount, or employee role.

1. **Setting Up Approval Levels**:
   - Define approval levels for each expense category. For instance, regular expenses may require manager approval, while high-cost expenses may need additional review by finance or senior management.
   - SAP Concur routes each expense report through the designated approval hierarchy, ensuring that only authorized individuals can approve specific types of expenses.
2. **Configuring Conditional Approvals**:
   - Set up conditional approvals for out-of-policy expenses, such as high-value transactions or expenses lacking receipts.
   - Conditional approvals ensure that policy exceptions receive appropriate scrutiny, helping to maintain expense policy integrity.

3. **Assigning Approvers Based on Role or Department**:
    - Configure approvers by employee role or department. For example, set up department heads to review expenses for their teams, while finance can review high-value or policy-exception expenses.
    - Role-based approval workflows streamline the process, allowing for efficient review and ensuring that the right people oversee expenses.
4. **Automating Notifications for Approvers**:
    - Enable notifications for approvers to ensure timely expense reviews. SAP Concur can notify approvers via email or app, allowing them to review pending expenses promptly.
    - Automated notifications keep the approval process moving efficiently, minimizing delays in reimbursement and policy enforcement.

Monitoring Compliance and Adjusting Expense Policies

SAP Concur's reporting tools allow organizations to monitor compliance with expense policies, track spending trends, and identify areas where policy adjustments may be needed.

1. **Generating Compliance Reports**:
   - o Use SAP Concur's compliance reports to review the frequency and types of policy violations, providing insight into common compliance issues.
   - o These reports highlight areas where employees frequently exceed limits or fail to follow documentation requirements, informing potential policy adjustments.
2. **Analyzing Spending Trends by Category**:
   - o Generate reports on spending by category, such as meals, lodging, or transportation, to identify high-cost areas.
   - o Analyzing spending trends helps organizations adjust limits or policies to align with current spending patterns, improving compliance and cost control.
3. **Adjusting Policies Based on Data Insights**:
   - o Use insights from compliance and spending reports to make data-driven adjustments to expense policies. For example, increase meal allowances for high-cost regions or adjust reimbursement limits based on feedback.
   - o Regularly adjusting policies ensures they remain relevant, practical, and aligned with the organization's budget goals.

4. **Providing Feedback to Employees**:
   - Share insights from compliance monitoring with employees, particularly if compliance rates are low or policy violations are common.
   - Providing feedback can improve adherence to expense policies, helping employees understand the importance of compliance and reducing policy violations.

Best Practices for Configuring Expense Policies

To maximize the effectiveness of expense policies in SAP Concur, follow these best practices:

1. **Maintain Clear and Concise Policies**:
   - Use simple language to make policies easy to understand, avoiding ambiguity or overly complex requirements.
   - Clear policies reduce confusion and make it easier for employees to comply with expense guidelines.
2. **Regularly Review and Update Policies**:
   - Schedule regular reviews of expense policies to ensure they reflect current travel costs, vendor agreements, and organizational goals.
   - Updating policies regularly helps maintain compliance and ensures

employees can follow practical, relevant guidelines.

3. **Train Employees on Policy Requirements**:
   - Provide training on expense policy requirements and the importance of compliance, highlighting any recent updates or changes.
   - Educating employees on policies improves adherence and minimizes the risk of policy violations.

4. **Encourage Feedback from Employees**:
   - Encourage employees to share their experiences and challenges with expense policies. This feedback can provide valuable insights into potential policy adjustments.
   - Employee feedback ensures policies are practical, balancing organizational goals with employee needs.

Conclusion

Configuring expense policies in SAP Concur allows organizations to enforce spending guidelines, manage costs, and streamline the expense reporting process. By following the steps in this chapter, organizations can create and enforce comprehensive policies that support compliance and efficiency.

In the next chapter, we'll explore the process of submitting and managing expense reports in SAP Concur, guiding employees through capturing expenses, attaching receipts, and completing the submission process.

This chapter provides a comprehensive guide to configuring expense policies in SAP Concur, helping organizations create clear, enforceable rules for managing expenses.

Chapter 10: Capturing and Submitting Expenses

Introduction

Capturing and submitting expenses in SAP Concur is a fundamental process for employees who travel or incur business-related expenses. This process involves recording expenses accurately, attaching receipts, and ensuring that submissions comply with company policies. In this chapter, we'll guide readers through the steps to capture and submit expenses in SAP Concur, covering best practices for accuracy, policy compliance, and efficient submission.

Overview of the Expense Submission Process

In SAP Concur, the expense submission process is designed to be user-friendly and efficient. Employees can capture expenses using various methods, organize them into reports, and submit for approval. The key steps involved in capturing and submitting expenses are:

1. **Recording Individual Expenses**: Enter expense details, such as date, amount, and purpose, to create an accurate record.
2. **Uploading Receipts**: Attach receipts to each expense, either by uploading images or using the mobile app's capture function.

3. **Organizing Expenses into Reports**: Group expenses into reports for submission, such as "October Client Meeting Expenses" or "Annual Conference Trip."
4. **Submitting for Approval**: Once the report is complete, submit it for manager approval in compliance with company policies.

Step 1: Recording Expenses

SAP Concur allows employees to capture expenses manually, through corporate credit card integration, or by using OCR (Optical Character Recognition) technology to scan receipts. Each method ensures accurate record-keeping and streamlines the submission process.

1. **Manual Entry**:
   - Access the **Expense** tab in SAP Concur and select **Create New Expense** to begin entering details manually.
   - Fill in key information, such as **Expense Type** (e.g., meals, transportation), **Date**, **Amount**, **Vendor Name**, and **Purpose** of the expense.
2. **Using Corporate Credit Card Integration**:
   - For employees with a corporate credit card linked to SAP Concur, charges automatically populate in the system.

- Go to the **Available Expenses** section to view these transactions, assign each to an expense report, and categorize them (e.g., "Hotel – Business Trip").
- Automatically populated transactions minimize data entry and ensure accurate tracking of company-paid expenses.

3. **Using Receipt Capture with OCR**:
   - SAP Concur's OCR technology allows employees to upload receipts via mobile or web. The system scans the receipt, extracting details like date, amount, and vendor name.
   - OCR significantly reduces manual entry, making it easy to submit accurate expense data with minimal effort.

Step 2: Attaching Receipts to Expenses

Attaching receipts is essential for expense verification and compliance. SAP Concur offers multiple options for attaching receipts, ensuring flexibility and ease of use.

1. **Uploading Receipts via Desktop**:
   - After entering an expense, click **Attach Receipt** to upload a digital receipt file (e.g., PDF, JPEG).
   - Select the file from your computer and upload it to the corresponding expense.

SAP Concur associates the receipt with the expense for seamless record-keeping.

2. **Capturing Receipts with the Mobile App**:
    o Use the SAP Concur mobile app to capture receipts on the go. Open the app, select **Capture Receipt**, and take a photo of the receipt.
    o The app saves the receipt image and attaches it to the relevant expense. OCR will process the details automatically, reducing manual data entry.

3. **Emailing Receipts to SAP Concur**:
    o Employees can forward email receipts directly to SAP Concur using a designated email address (e.g., receipts@concur.com).
    o SAP Concur associates emailed receipts with the user's account, making them accessible in the **Available Receipts** section, where they can be linked to specific expenses.

4. **Matching Receipts with Expenses**:
    o For expenses where multiple receipts may be relevant (e.g., hotel stays with various charges), ensure that each expense has a matching receipt.
    o SAP Concur flags any expenses missing required receipts, prompting users to complete their submissions for compliance.

Step 3: Organizing Expenses into Reports

Creating organized expense reports simplifies the submission process for both employees and approvers. Reports group related expenses, such as all expenses from a single business trip, into a single document for approval.

1. **Creating a New Expense Report**:
   - Navigate to the **Expense** tab and select **Create New Report**. Enter a report name, such as "November Client Visit," and add basic details, including the **Start Date**, **End Date**, and **Business Purpose**.
   - SAP Concur allows users to save draft reports, enabling them to add expenses over time and submit the completed report later.
2. **Adding Expenses to a Report**:
   - Select the **Add Expense** option to include individual expenses in the report. Choose from manually entered expenses, corporate card charges, or receipts captured via mobile.
   - Each expense item appears within the report, providing a consolidated view of all related expenses for easy review.

3. **Categorizing Expenses**:
    o SAP Concur categorizes expenses according to policy guidelines, such as "Meals," "Transportation," or "Lodging."
    o Accurate categorization ensures that expenses align with company policies, and it simplifies approval for managers.
4. **Reviewing Policy Compliance**:
    o As expenses are added, SAP Concur checks them against the organization's policies, flagging any non-compliant items. For example, if a meal expense exceeds the daily limit, the system highlights the item for review.
    o Users can adjust flagged expenses to align with policy, add justifications for policy exceptions, or submit them for conditional approval if necessary.

Step 4: Submitting the Expense Report for Approval

Once the expense report is complete, employees can submit it for manager approval. SAP Concur routes the report through the approval workflow, ensuring compliance checks before reimbursement processing.

1. **Final Review of the Report**:
    o Review each expense in the report, verifying that all required details and receipts are included. SAP Concur

provides a summary view of each item for quick review.
   o Ensure that flagged expenses are resolved, and add any necessary justifications or comments for items that require additional review.

2. **Submitting the Report**:
   o Click **Submit Report** to initiate the approval process. SAP Concur notifies the designated approver(s) automatically, providing them with a link to review and approve the report.
   o Users receive a confirmation once the report is submitted, along with updates on approval status throughout the process.

3. **Tracking the Approval Process**:
   o SAP Concur's **Report Status** feature allows employees to monitor the status of their submitted reports, such as "Pending Approval" or "Approved."
   o If the approver requests adjustments or additional documentation, SAP Concur notifies the user, enabling them to make the necessary updates and resubmit.

Best Practices for Capturing and Submitting Expenses

Following best practices for capturing and submitting expenses helps streamline the process, ensures compliance, and avoids delays in reimbursement.

1. **Capture Expenses Promptly**:
   - Record expenses as they occur, ideally using the mobile app for real-time capture. Prompt recording helps maintain accuracy and minimizes the risk of missing details or receipts.
2. **Use the Mobile App for Convenience**:
   - The SAP Concur mobile app simplifies capturing receipts and tracking expenses on the go, particularly during business travel. Leverage mobile features to capture expenses immediately and upload receipts from any location.
3. **Check Policy Limits and Requirements**:
   - Familiarize yourself with company policies to ensure that expenses align with spending limits and receipt requirements. Checking policies reduces the likelihood of flagged items and saves time during submission.
4. **Organize Reports by Project or Trip**:
   - Group related expenses into a single report, such as "Annual Sales Meeting" or "December Training." Organized

reports make it easier for approvers to review and understand expenses in context.

5. **Resolve Flagged Items Before Submission**:
   o Address any policy violations flagged by SAP Concur, either by adjusting the expense or providing a justification. Resolving issues before submission minimizes delays and increases the likelihood of swift approval.

6. **Track Approval Status Regularly**:
   o Stay updated on your report's status to ensure that any requested adjustments are handled promptly. This helps avoid delays in reimbursement and maintains a smooth expense reporting process.

Common Issues and Troubleshooting in Expense Submission

While SAP Concur streamlines expense submission, certain issues may arise, such as missing receipts or policy violations. Here's how to address common challenges:

1. **Missing Receipts**:
   o If a receipt is missing, use the **Receipt Affidavit** option if your company policy permits it. This option allows employees

to acknowledge the missing receipt and explain the circumstances.

- For expenses requiring additional documentation, such as hotel bills with multiple charges, ensure each item is detailed and that the primary receipt reflects the total expense.

2. **Policy Violation Flags**:
   - Review flagged items to determine the cause, such as exceeding spending limits or selecting a non-preferred vendor. Adjust the entry or provide a detailed explanation for the violation if it's unavoidable.
   - For expenses needing special approval, SAP Concur routes the flagged item to a higher-level approver, ensuring compliance while accommodating necessary exceptions.

3. **Rejected Expense Reports**:
   - If a report is rejected, SAP Concur notifies the user with specific feedback from the approver. Address the feedback, correct any errors, and resubmit the report.
   - Rejections often occur due to missing receipts or non-compliance with policy. Addressing these issues ensures that future reports align with approval standards.

4. **Corporate Card Transaction Delays**:
   - Occasionally, corporate card transactions may experience delays in appearing within SAP Concur. Wait a day or two for charges to populate, or manually enter the expense if the delay persists.
   - If corporate card transactions repeatedly fail to sync, contact SAP Concur support to investigate potential integration issues.

Conclusion

Capturing and submitting expenses in SAP Concur is a straightforward process when employees follow clear steps for recording expenses, attaching receipts, and organizing reports. By using the tools available within SAP Concur, employees can maintain accuracy, ensure compliance with company policies, and simplify the approval process.

In the next chapter, we'll cover **Automating Receipt Management**.

This chapter provides a detailed guide to capturing and submitting expenses in SAP Concur, helping employees follow best practices and maintain compliance.

Chapter 11: Automating Receipt Management

Introduction

Automating receipt management in SAP Concur streamlines the expense reporting process, reduces errors, and ensures compliance with company policies. By using tools such as Optical Character Recognition (OCR), mobile receipt capture, and automated matching, SAP Concur makes it easy for employees to upload, organize, and attach receipts to expenses. This chapter will guide readers through SAP Concur's receipt management features, focusing on the tools available for capturing and matching receipts, the benefits of automation, and best practices for maintaining accurate and compliant records.

The Benefits of Automating Receipt Management

Automating receipt management offers numerous benefits for both employees and the organization. It simplifies expense submission, enhances policy compliance, and improves accuracy in expense reporting. Key benefits include:

1. **Time Savings**: Automated receipt capture and data extraction reduce the need for manual entry, allowing employees to complete expense submissions quickly.

2. **Increased Accuracy**: Automated tools minimize human error by accurately extracting data from receipts, ensuring that information such as date, amount, and vendor name are captured correctly.
3. **Enhanced Compliance**: Automated receipt checks ensure that each expense meets documentation requirements, reducing the likelihood of policy violations.
4. **Improved Record Keeping**: With all receipts stored digitally, organizations can maintain a comprehensive, searchable record of expenses, making audits and compliance reviews more manageable.

Step 1: Capturing Receipts with the SAP Concur Mobile App

The SAP Concur mobile app is an essential tool for receipt management, allowing employees to capture and upload receipts directly from their smartphones. This feature is especially useful for employees on the go, ensuring they can submit receipts as expenses are incurred.

1. **Accessing the Receipt Capture Tool**:
   o Open the SAP Concur mobile app and navigate to the **Expenses** tab. Select **Capture Receipt** to activate the camera.

- Align the receipt in the camera frame, ensuring the entire document is visible and that key information (e.g., date, amount, vendor) is clear.

2. **Capturing the Receipt Image**:
   - Take a photo of the receipt and confirm that the image quality is adequate. SAP Concur's OCR technology will extract information from the receipt, so clear images are essential for accurate data capture.
   - If needed, retake the photo to ensure clarity, especially if the receipt includes detailed line items or small print.

3. **Automatic Data Extraction Using OCR**:
   - Once the receipt is captured, SAP Concur uses OCR to extract key details, including date, amount, and vendor name.
   - The extracted information populates the relevant fields automatically, reducing the need for manual entry. Employees can review the data for accuracy and make adjustments if necessary.

4. **Saving Receipts for Future Use**:
   - Captured receipts are saved in the **Available Receipts** section of SAP Concur, where they can be accessed later and attached to relevant expenses.

- This feature allows employees to capture receipts in real-time and link them to expense reports at their convenience.

Step 2: Uploading Digital Receipts via Email

For digital receipts, such as those received via email for online purchases or travel bookings, SAP Concur offers a simple email forwarding feature. Employees can forward digital receipts directly to SAP Concur, where they are processed and stored.

1. **Setting Up Email Receipt Forwarding**:
   - Each SAP Concur user receives a unique email address for forwarding receipts (e.g., receipts@concur.com).
   - Employees should save this email address to easily forward digital receipts directly from their inbox.
2. **Forwarding Email Receipts**:
   - Forward the email receipt to the SAP Concur email address. SAP Concur automatically recognizes the receipt and stores it in the user's **Available Receipts** section.
   - When forwarding, ensure the receipt is the main content of the email or in an attachment (e.g., PDF), as this improves data extraction accuracy.

3. **Processing and Storing the Receipt**:
   - ○ SAP Concur processes the forwarded receipt using OCR to extract relevant details, such as date, vendor, and amount.
   - ○ Digital receipts are then saved in the user's account, ready to be attached to expense reports as needed.

Step 3: Attaching Receipts to Expenses in SAP Concur

Once receipts are captured or uploaded, they can be attached to individual expenses, either manually or through automated matching. SAP Concur's matching feature associates receipts with expenses based on data such as date, amount, and vendor.

1. **Viewing Available Receipts**:
   - ○ In the **Expenses** tab, access the **Available Receipts** section to view all saved receipts.
   - ○ Each receipt is stored with basic information extracted through OCR, making it easy to locate specific receipts by date or vendor.
2. **Attaching Receipts Manually**:
   - ○ For each expense item, select **Attach Receipt** and choose from the available receipts.

- Manual attachment ensures that each expense is documented, and it allows employees to verify that the correct receipt is attached to the right expense.
3. **Using Automatic Receipt Matching**:
   - SAP Concur's automatic matching feature associates receipts with expenses based on matching data (e.g., amount, date).
   - Employees can review matched receipts and confirm their accuracy. Automatic matching simplifies the submission process and reduces the risk of attaching incorrect receipts.
4. **Adding Multiple Receipts to a Single Expense**:
   - For complex expenses that require multiple receipts, such as hotel bills covering multiple nights or expenses with itemized charges, SAP Concur allows employees to attach multiple receipts to one expense entry.
   - This feature ensures complete documentation and improves compliance with receipt requirements.

Step 4: Managing Receipt Requirements and Compliance

Receipt requirements are a key part of expense policy compliance. SAP Concur enforces receipt policies automatically, ensuring that each expense meets documentation standards before submission.

1. **Defining Receipt Requirements**:
   - Configure receipt requirements in SAP Concur based on organizational policies, such as requiring receipts for expenses above a specific amount.
   - Common requirements include receipts for expenses over $25 or receipts for meals, lodging, and transportation expenses.
2. **Setting Compliance Flags for Missing Receipts**:
   - SAP Concur flags expenses that lack required receipts, notifying employees to attach the necessary documentation.
   - Compliance flags help employees address missing receipts before submission, reducing delays in the approval process.
3. **Using Receipt Affidavits for Lost Receipts**:
   - For instances where a receipt is lost or unavailable, some organizations allow employees to submit a **Receipt Affidavit** in place of the receipt.
   - SAP Concur offers an affidavit option, allowing employees to acknowledge missing receipts and provide an explanation. This feature supports compliance while accommodating occasional exceptions.

Step 5: Organizing and Storing Digital Receipts

SAP Concur's receipt storage feature provides a centralized repository for all digital receipts, making it easy for employees and administrators to access documentation for expenses, audits, and reporting.

1. **Centralized Receipt Storage**:
   - All captured and uploaded receipts are stored in the user's **Available Receipts** section, providing a searchable archive.
   - Centralized storage simplifies record-keeping, making it easy to locate receipts for specific expenses, dates, or vendors.
2. **Using Receipts for Audits and Compliance**:
   - Stored receipts are accessible for audits, allowing administrators to review expense documentation quickly.
   - SAP Concur's search function makes it easy to retrieve receipts based on criteria such as amount, date, or vendor, supporting efficient audit processes.
3. **Archiving and Retrieving Historical Receipts**:
   - SAP Concur archives receipts for a designated period based on organizational retention policies. Archived receipts are accessible for historical reference, audits, or compliance reviews.

- o This feature ensures that receipts remain available for a specified duration, meeting legal and regulatory requirements for record-keeping.

Best Practices for Automating Receipt Management

Automating receipt management in SAP Concur is most effective when combined with best practices for capturing, organizing, and storing receipts. These practices ensure efficiency, accuracy, and compliance.

1. **Capture Receipts Immediately**:
   - o Encourage employees to capture receipts as expenses are incurred, using the mobile app or email forwarding for quick submission.
   - o Immediate capture minimizes the risk of losing receipts and improves the accuracy of expense entries.
2. **Ensure Clear Receipt Images**:
   - o When capturing receipts with the mobile app, ensure that the images are clear and legible. SAP Concur's OCR requires high-quality images to extract accurate information.
   - o Blurry or incomplete images may lead to data extraction errors, resulting in manual corrections.

3. **Review Extracted Data for Accuracy**:
   - After capturing or uploading a receipt, review the automatically extracted data (e.g., amount, date) for accuracy. SAP Concur's OCR is highly accurate, but occasional errors may occur.
   - Promptly correcting any data discrepancies ensures accurate and compliant expense reports.
4. **Follow Organizational Receipt Policies**:
   - Familiarize employees with receipt requirements, such as when receipts are mandatory and what information they should contain.
   - Clear guidelines on receipt policies improve compliance and reduce the need for manual oversight during the approval process.
5. **Use Automated Matching to Streamline Submission**:
   - Encourage employees to use SAP Concur's automatic matching feature, which saves time and minimizes the risk of attaching incorrect receipts.
   - Automated matching provides a seamless experience, especially for employees with multiple expenses, such as during business trips.

6. **Leverage Digital Storage for Audit Readiness**:
    - o SAP Concur's centralized receipt storage supports audit readiness, making it easy to retrieve documentation for expense verification.
    - o Regular audits of stored receipts can ensure that all expenses are properly documented and compliant with organizational policies.

Common Issues and Troubleshooting for Receipt Management

While SAP Concur's automated receipt management is designed to be user-friendly, some common issues may arise. Here's how to address typical challenges.

1. **Unclear or Low-Quality Receipt Images**:
    - o If a receipt image is unclear or incomplete, retake the photo in a well-lit area. Ensure the receipt is flat and that all text is legible.
    - o Encourage employees to verify the clarity of each image before submission, particularly when using the mobile app.
2. **Incorrect Data Extraction by OCR**:
    - o Occasionally, OCR may misinterpret information on receipts, especially if fonts are unclear or if the receipt is damaged.

- o Review extracted data carefully and make manual corrections as needed to ensure accuracy before attaching receipts to expenses.
3. **Duplicate Receipts**:
   - o Duplicate receipts may occur if a receipt is captured both via mobile and email. SAP Concur alerts users to potential duplicates, allowing them to remove redundant entries.
   - o Encourage employees to check for duplicates before submitting expenses to streamline the report review process.
4. **Missing Receipts for Required Expenses**:
   - o If a required receipt is missing, employees can submit a Receipt Affidavit if allowed by company policy. This option ensures compliance and allows the expense to proceed without unnecessary delays.
   - o For persistent issues with missing receipts, consider reinforcing training on receipt capture best practices to improve compliance.

Conclusion

Automating receipt management in SAP Concur significantly improves the efficiency, accuracy, and compliance of the expense reporting process. By leveraging tools such as OCR, mobile capture, and automated matching, employees can streamline the process of documenting expenses and ensure that all receipts meet organizational requirements.

In the next chapter, we'll explore the approval workflow for expense reports, focusing on the roles of managers and finance teams in reviewing, approving, and processing reimbursements.

This chapter provides a comprehensive guide to automating receipt management in SAP Concur, helping employees capture and submit receipts accurately and efficiently.

Chapter 12: Expense Approval Workflow

Introduction

The expense approval workflow in SAP Concur is designed to ensure that submitted expenses comply with company policies before reimbursement. This workflow enables managers and finance teams to review, approve, or reject expenses efficiently while enforcing compliance and controlling costs. In this chapter, we will cover the steps involved in the approval process, including routing expenses to approvers, managing policy compliance, and understanding approval levels. Additionally, we will discuss best practices for approvers to streamline the workflow and maintain accurate records.

The Importance of an Effective Approval Workflow

An effective expense approval workflow is essential for organizations aiming to:

1. **Ensure Policy Compliance**: By reviewing each expense, managers can verify compliance with company policies, ensuring that only allowable expenses are reimbursed.
2. **Control Costs**: Approvers can identify unnecessary or excessive spending, helping

organizations manage travel and business expenses.

3. **Enhance Transparency and Accountability**: The approval process creates a clear record of who approved each expense, fostering accountability.
4. **Maintain Efficiency**: Automated workflows streamline the approval process, reducing delays and improving the reimbursement timeline.

Overview of the Expense Approval Workflow in SAP Concur

SAP Concur's expense approval workflow is configurable to meet organizational needs. It typically includes the following steps:

1. **Expense Report Submission**: Employees submit completed expense reports, which include captured receipts, itemized expenses, and any necessary justifications for policy exceptions.
2. **Automated Policy Checks**: SAP Concur runs automatic checks to flag policy violations, providing approvers with an initial compliance assessment.
3. **Routing to Approvers**: The system routes expense reports to designated approvers, usually based on employee role, department, or expense type.
4. **Approver Review**: Approvers review each expense item for accuracy, compliance, and

completeness, approving or rejecting items as necessary.

5. **Final Approval or Rejection**: Once reviewed, the report is either fully approved for reimbursement or rejected, requiring further action from the employee.

Step 1: Configuring Approval Levels in SAP Concur

Before the approval workflow begins, it's essential to configure the levels of approval within SAP Concur. Approval levels can be set based on expense type, amount, employee role, or department, allowing organizations to define the appropriate level of review for each type of expense.

1. **Setting Approval Thresholds**:
    o   Configure thresholds for each level of approval based on the cost of expenses. For example, routine expenses under $100 might only require a manager's approval, while larger expenses require additional review from finance.
    o   SAP Concur allows for multiple levels of approval, so high-value or out-of-policy expenses can receive extra scrutiny.
2. **Assigning Role-Based Approvals**:
    o   Configure approvers based on employee roles, such as department heads or

senior managers, who are responsible for reviewing their team's expenses.
- Role-based approvals ensure that the right individuals have oversight of expenses, maintaining accountability across departments.

3. **Defining Conditional Approvals**:
    - For out-of-policy expenses, configure conditional approvals that route these items to higher-level approvers. For example, an expense exceeding a policy limit for meals might require a secondary approval from the finance department.
    - Conditional approvals allow flexibility in handling exceptions while ensuring that all policy deviations receive adequate review.

Step 2: Reviewing Submitted Expense Reports

Once an expense report is submitted, SAP Concur routes it to the designated approver(s) for review. The review process includes checking for policy compliance, accuracy, and completeness. Here's a closer look at the steps involved in reviewing reports.

1. **Accessing Expense Reports**:
    - Approvers can access submitted reports from their **Approvals** tab within SAP Concur, where they see a list of pending

expense reports along with basic information, such as the submitter's name, report name, and total amount.
- o Approvers can prioritize reviews based on urgency, focusing on high-value reports or those nearing a reimbursement deadline.

2. **Checking for Policy Compliance**:
   - o SAP Concur flags any policy violations automatically, providing approvers with a summary of out-of-policy items. Violations may include expenses exceeding category limits, missing receipts, or using non-preferred vendors.
   - o Approvers can review the flagged items and determine if they require additional justification or adjustments.

3. **Verifying Receipt Attachments**:
   - o Approvers check that each expense has a corresponding receipt attached as required by company policy. SAP Concur highlights missing or incomplete receipts, allowing approvers to request corrections from the employee.
   - o Accurate receipt documentation is essential for compliance and record-keeping, making this an important step in the review process.

4. **Evaluating Justifications for Exceptions**:
    o   For any out-of-policy expenses, approvers review the employee's justification. Examples might include selecting a higher-cost hotel due to location or a meal expense that exceeded the allowance due to an extended meeting.
    o   Approvers can either accept the justification and approve the item or request additional information if the justification is insufficient.

Step 3: Approving or Rejecting Expense Items

Once the review is complete, approvers can either approve or reject each expense item within the report. This step ensures that only compliant expenses proceed to reimbursement.

1. **Approving Items**:
    o   Approvers approve compliant items individually or approve the entire report if all items meet policy standards.
    o   Approved items are forwarded to the next level in the workflow, if applicable, or proceed to reimbursement processing.
2. **Rejecting Non-Compliant Items**:
    o   For expenses that do not meet company policy or lack sufficient documentation,

approvers can reject specific items within the report.

- o SAP Concur allows approvers to provide reasons for rejection, which are visible to the employee. Clear feedback helps employees correct and resubmit rejected items promptly.

3. **Partial Approvals**:
    - o In cases where some items in a report are compliant and others are not, approvers can issue a partial approval. Approved items proceed to reimbursement, while rejected items return to the employee for adjustment.
    - o Partial approvals streamline the reimbursement process, ensuring timely reimbursement for compliant items without delaying the entire report.

Step 4: Managing Notifications and Communication

SAP Concur provides automated notifications throughout the approval process, ensuring that both employees and approvers stay informed of report status and any required actions.

1. **Automated Notifications for Approvers**:
    - o Approvers receive notifications when a new expense report is submitted, prompting them to review it.

Notifications can be sent via email or app alerts, ensuring that reports are reviewed promptly.

- o Regular notifications help approvers stay on top of their tasks, reducing delays in the workflow.

2. **Employee Notifications for Rejections or Adjustments**:
   - o If an expense item is rejected, the employee receives a notification with feedback from the approver. This allows them to address the issue, such as attaching a missing receipt or providing additional justification.
   - o Notifications streamline communication and reduce back-and-forth, allowing employees to quickly make the necessary adjustments and resubmit.

3. **Tracking Approval Status**:
   - o Both employees and approvers can track the status of an expense report within SAP Concur, viewing updates such as "Pending Approval," "Approved," or "Rejected."
   - o Transparent status updates improve accountability and keep the workflow organized, ensuring everyone involved knows the report's progress.

Step 5: Processing Approved Reports for Reimbursement

Once an expense report has been fully approved, it proceeds to the reimbursement phase. SAP Concur automates much of the reimbursement process, sending approved reports to the finance team or accounting system for payment.

1. **Automated Routing to Finance**:
   - Approved expense reports are automatically forwarded to the finance team for payment processing. This step ensures a seamless transition from approval to reimbursement.
   - SAP Concur integrates with most accounting systems, enabling data transfer and expediting the reimbursement timeline.
2. **Reimbursement Processing**:
   - The finance team verifies that all reports are fully approved and compliant with organizational policies before issuing reimbursement.
   - Reimbursements are typically processed within the established payroll cycle or as per the organization's policy, ensuring employees receive timely payments.

3. **Recording and Archiving Reports**:
   - SAP Concur stores approved reports and related receipts in its digital archive, providing a complete record of expenses for future reference, audits, or compliance checks.
   - Archived reports are searchable, making it easy for finance or HR teams to access expense records as needed.

Best Practices for Managing Expense Approvals

A well-managed approval workflow improves efficiency and compliance. Here are best practices for approvers to ensure a smooth and effective process.

1. **Review Expenses Promptly**:
   - Timely review of expense reports helps maintain efficiency and avoids delays in reimbursement. Approvers should prioritize review tasks and respond to reports within established timelines.
   - Prompt reviews prevent backlog and ensure that employees are reimbursed without unnecessary delays.
2. **Provide Clear Feedback for Rejected Items**:
   - When rejecting an expense, provide specific feedback so employees understand the issue and can make necessary adjustments.

- Clear feedback reduces misunderstandings, streamlining the resubmission process and encouraging compliance.
3. **Use SAP Concur's Mobile App for Flexibility**:
    - The SAP Concur mobile app allows approvers to review and approve expenses on the go, making it convenient to manage approvals without needing to log in to a desktop system.
    - Mobile approval helps keep the workflow moving and improves responsiveness, especially for time-sensitive reports.
4. **Maintain Consistency in Approvals**:
    - Apply policies consistently when approving or rejecting expenses. Consistency reinforces policy adherence and ensures that all employees are held to the same standards.
    - If policy changes are needed, communicate updates clearly to avoid confusion and improve compliance.
5. **Monitor and Report on Approval Metrics**:
    - Regularly monitor approval metrics, such as average approval time, compliance rates, and rejection reasons. Analyzing these metrics can highlight areas for improvement and inform policy adjustments.

- Reporting metrics helps organizations assess the effectiveness of their approval process and identify potential efficiency gains.

Common Issues and Troubleshooting in Approval Workflow

Occasional issues may arise in the approval workflow. Here's how to address common challenges effectively.

1. **Delayed Approvals**:
   - If approvals are delayed, approvers may need reminders. SAP Concur allows for automated reminders to keep the workflow on track.
   - Consider configuring escalation paths for urgent reports, routing them to an alternate approver if the primary approver is unavailable.
2. **Frequent Policy Violations**:
   - If reports frequently include out-of-policy expenses, consider reviewing and updating the policy to ensure it aligns with current business needs.
   - Regular training on policy requirements can also improve compliance and reduce policy violations in expense reports.

3. **Incomplete Expense Documentation**:
    - In cases of incomplete documentation, approvers can request missing information before proceeding with approval. SAP Concur's notifications provide employees with clear instructions on the required adjustments.
    - Reinforcing the importance of complete submissions in training sessions can help employees submit compliant reports consistently.

Conclusion

An effective expense approval workflow in SAP Concur helps organizations maintain compliance, control costs, and ensure timely reimbursement. By configuring appropriate approval levels, managing policy compliance, and using SAP Concur's automation tools, managers can streamline the process and improve accuracy in expense reporting.

In the next chapter, we'll cover **Expense Auditing and Compliance**.

This chapter provides a thorough guide to managing the expense approval workflow in SAP Concur, helping organizations maintain control and ensure compliance.

Chapter 13: Expense Auditing and Compliance

Introduction

Expense auditing and compliance are essential components of corporate expense management. They ensure that expenses align with company policies, regulatory requirements, and financial controls, protecting the organization from fraud, errors, and excessive spending. SAP Concur's auditing features simplify this process by automating policy enforcement, highlighting exceptions, and providing tools for thorough expense review. In this chapter, we'll explore how to conduct expense audits, enforce compliance effectively, and leverage SAP Concur's tools to streamline these activities.

The Importance of Expense Auditing and Compliance

Effective expense auditing and compliance practices offer several benefits for organizations:

1. **Fraud Prevention**: Audits help detect and prevent fraudulent expenses, ensuring that only legitimate costs are reimbursed.
2. **Policy Enforcement**: Auditing enforces adherence to corporate expense policies, reducing out-of-policy spending.

3. **Cost Control**: Audits identify excessive or unnecessary spending, allowing organizations to manage expenses proactively.
4. **Regulatory Compliance**: By ensuring proper documentation and adherence to policies, audits help organizations meet regulatory standards and prepare for external audits.

Types of Expense Audits

SAP Concur allows for multiple types of audits to meet different compliance needs, including pre-approval, post-approval, and random audits.

1. **Pre-Approval Audits**:
   - Pre-approval audits occur before an expense report is fully approved. During this stage, approvers review each expense for policy compliance and completeness.
   - These audits focus on identifying issues before they reach the reimbursement stage, allowing for prompt adjustments and corrections.
2. **Post-Approval Audits**:
   - Post-approval audits take place after expenses have been approved and reimbursed. This type of audit typically involves reviewing a sample of expenses to ensure long-term compliance.

- Post-approval audits allow organizations to identify patterns or recurring issues and refine policies or practices accordingly.

3. **Random Audits**:
   - Random audits are conducted periodically and involve reviewing a sample of expense reports. Random selection helps organizations gain an unbiased view of compliance and identify potential areas for improvement.
   - These audits serve as a deterrent to fraud and non-compliance by ensuring that employees are aware of potential review.

4. **Targeted Audits**:
   - Targeted audits focus on specific expense categories, departments, or types of spending. For example, a targeted audit might review all travel expenses or high-value entertainment expenses.
   - These audits provide insights into particular spending areas and help refine policy guidelines for those categories.

Step 1: Setting Up Audit Rules in SAP Concur

Audit rules in SAP Concur help automate the identification of potential compliance issues. By defining these rules, organizations can streamline the audit process and ensure consistent enforcement of policies.

1. **Defining Audit Criteria**:
   - Establish criteria for identifying policy violations, such as expenses exceeding allowable limits, missing receipts, or out-of-policy spending.
   - SAP Concur allows organizations to customize rules based on expense type, amount, location, or employee role, providing flexibility to address specific compliance needs.
2. **Configuring Automated Audit Flags**:
   - SAP Concur's automated audit flags highlight non-compliant expenses, making it easy for auditors to focus on items requiring additional review.
   - Examples of automated flags include missing documentation, duplicate expenses, or expenses that exceed category limits.
3. **Applying Conditional Approval for Flagged Expenses**:
   - Expenses flagged by audit rules can be routed for additional approval or secondary review before reimbursement.
   - This conditional approval process helps enforce compliance for high-risk items, ensuring that flagged expenses receive thorough scrutiny.

4. **Customizing Audit Policies for Departments or Locations**:
    - SAP Concur enables organizations to configure audit policies based on departments, regions, or travel types, allowing for customized compliance enforcement.
    - For example, higher meal allowances can be set for employees traveling to high-cost cities, and stricter policies can be enforced for departments with high travel budgets.

Step 2: Conducting Expense Audits in SAP Concur

Once audit rules are in place, SAP Concur provides a streamlined platform for conducting audits, from reviewing flagged items to verifying documentation.

1. **Reviewing Flagged Expenses**:
    - Auditors can access a list of flagged expenses from the **Audit** dashboard, where they see all items requiring review.
    - Each flagged item includes details such as the policy violation, employee name, and expense type, allowing auditors to prioritize reviews based on the severity of the issue.

2. **Verifying Documentation**:
    - For flagged expenses requiring receipts, auditors can review attached documents to ensure compliance with receipt requirements.
    - If documentation is incomplete or illegible, auditors can request additional information or clarification from the employee.
3. **Evaluating Justifications for Out-of-Policy Items**:
    - Some flagged expenses may include justifications from employees explaining why they exceed policy limits. Auditors can evaluate these justifications to determine if the expense is valid.
    - Auditors can approve the expense with justification or deny it if the justification does not meet policy standards.
4. **Checking for Duplicate Expenses**:
    - SAP Concur's system automatically flags potential duplicate expenses, such as two expenses with the same date and amount. Auditors can review these entries to confirm or reject duplicates.
    - Identifying duplicates helps prevent fraudulent or accidental duplicate reimbursements, improving expense integrity.

Step 3: Resolving Compliance Issues

Once the audit review is complete, auditors can take action to address any compliance issues, including requesting corrections, rejecting non-compliant expenses, or providing feedback.

1. **Requesting Adjustments from Employees**:
   o If a compliance issue can be corrected, auditors can request that the employee adjust the entry. For example, they may need to reduce the amount to comply with category limits or attach a missing receipt.
   o SAP Concur notifies employees of adjustment requests, allowing them to make corrections and resubmit the expense for review.
2. **Rejecting Non-Compliant Expenses**:
   o For expenses that cannot be corrected, auditors can reject the item, preventing reimbursement. SAP Concur records the rejection reason, and the employee is notified.
   o Rejecting non-compliant expenses enforces policy adherence and sets clear expectations for acceptable spending practices.

3. **Escalating High-Risk Issues**:
   - ○ If an expense raises significant concerns, such as potential fraud or a large out-of-policy amount, auditors can escalate the issue to management or finance for further investigation.
   - ○ Escalation helps address serious compliance risks and provides additional oversight for high-value or unusual expenses.
4. **Providing Feedback on Compliance Trends**:
   - ○ Auditors can provide feedback to managers or departments on recurring compliance issues. For instance, if a department frequently exceeds travel meal allowances, additional training or policy adjustments may be necessary.
   - ○ Feedback helps departments improve compliance and informs policy updates that better align with actual expenses.

Step 4: Reporting and Analyzing Audit Results

SAP Concur's reporting tools provide insights into audit outcomes, helping organizations understand compliance trends and identify areas for improvement.

1. **Generating Compliance Reports**:
   - ○ SAP Concur's compliance reports summarize audit findings, highlighting

areas such as policy violations, duplicate expenses, and missing receipts.

- Compliance reports help organizations assess the overall effectiveness of their expense policies and identify departments or categories with high non-compliance rates.

2. **Analyzing Common Policy Violations**:
   - Identify the most common types of policy violations, such as meal expenses exceeding limits or missing receipts for transportation.
   - Analyzing these trends helps organizations refine policies or provide additional guidance in areas with frequent issues.

3. **Tracking Audit Frequency and Coverage**:
   - Use SAP Concur's reporting tools to track the frequency of audits and the percentage of expenses reviewed. Regular auditing improves compliance, and tracking coverage ensures that all areas are sufficiently monitored.
   - If specific departments or expense categories have low audit coverage, consider increasing audit frequency for those areas.

4. **Measuring Cost Savings from Compliance**:
   - Compliance reports can quantify the cost savings achieved through expense

auditing, such as amounts recovered from rejected expenses or duplicates.
- o These insights demonstrate the value of the audit program and help justify the allocation of resources to compliance initiatives.

Step 5: Implementing Continuous Improvement in Expense Compliance

Ongoing improvement of expense policies and audit practices ensures that organizations maintain high compliance standards while adapting to evolving business needs.

1. **Refining Expense Policies Based on Audit Results**:
   - o Use audit findings to refine policies and update spending limits, receipt requirements, or preferred vendor guidelines.
   - o For instance, if high costs are identified for certain travel destinations, adjust travel allowances for those locations to improve policy alignment.
2. **Training Employees on Common Compliance Issues**:
   - o Conduct periodic training sessions to address recurring compliance issues highlighted in audit reports. Topics might

include submitting complete documentation, understanding policy limits, or managing corporate card expenses.

- Proactive training helps employees understand expectations, reducing the likelihood of policy violations.

3. **Automating Compliance Checks for Frequent Issues**:
    - Implement additional automated checks within SAP Concur for common policy violations, such as overspending on meals or missing receipts.
    - Automating these checks reduces manual review time and ensures consistent enforcement of policies across all expense reports.

4. **Engaging with Department Heads on Compliance Trends**:
    - Regularly share compliance insights with department heads, highlighting trends, improvement areas, and policy updates relevant to their teams.
    - Engaging departments in compliance efforts promotes accountability and helps ensure that all areas of the organization support policy adherence.

Best Practices for Effective Expense Auditing and Compliance

To maintain a robust auditing and compliance program, follow these best practices:

1. **Conduct Random Audits Regularly**:
    - o Random audits provide an unbiased view of expense compliance and help detect potential issues across the organization.
    - o Regular random audits keep employees aware that expenses may be reviewed at any time, reinforcing adherence to policy.
2. **Implement Tiered Audits for High-Value Expenses**:
    - o For high-cost or high-risk expenses, conduct tiered audits that require review by multiple approvers or auditors.
    - o Tiered audits ensure that large expenses receive sufficient oversight, reducing the risk of fraud or policy abuse.
3. **Communicate Audit Results Transparently**:
    - o Share audit results with employees and departments to reinforce compliance and provide constructive feedback.
    - o Transparent communication improves understanding of policies and helps employees align their spending with organizational expectations.

4. **Continuously Update Policies Based on Audit Insights**:
   - Use audit data to keep policies current, adapting them to reflect changes in business needs, travel costs, and employee behavior.
   - Regular policy updates based on audit insights ensure that policies remain relevant, practical, and enforceable.

Conclusion

Effective expense auditing and compliance are crucial for protecting an organization's finances, enforcing policies, and preventing fraud. SAP Concur's auditing tools allow organizations to automate many aspects of this process, from identifying policy violations to generating compliance reports. By following this chapter's guidelines, organizations can maintain a proactive compliance program, ensuring that all expenses align with company standards.

In the next chapter, we will explore **Introduction to Concur Invoice**.

This chapter provides a comprehensive guide to expense auditing and compliance, helping organizations enforce policies, prevent fraud, and improve accountability.

Chapter 14: Introduction to Concur Invoice

Introduction

Concur Invoice is SAP Concur's solution for automating invoice processing, helping organizations manage supplier invoices efficiently, reduce processing time, and improve compliance. With Concur Invoice, companies can streamline the entire invoice lifecycle, from capture to approval and payment, reducing the need for manual data entry and minimizing the risk of errors. This chapter will introduce you to Concur Invoice, covering its features, benefits, and the basics of setting up and using the tool to manage invoices effectively.

The Importance of Invoice Automation

Manual invoice processing can be time-consuming, error-prone, and costly. Automating the process with Concur Invoice offers several key advantages:

1. **Improved Efficiency**: Automating data capture and workflows speeds up invoice processing, reducing turnaround times and freeing staff from repetitive tasks.
2. **Enhanced Accuracy**: Concur Invoice's data extraction capabilities reduce manual entry errors, ensuring that data is accurately recorded.

3. **Better Compliance**: Built-in compliance checks help organizations enforce policies for purchase orders, vendor approvals, and spending limits.
4. **Increased Visibility**: Real-time reporting and tracking provide better visibility into invoices, helping organizations manage cash flow and budget more effectively.

Key Features of Concur Invoice

Concur Invoice provides a range of features designed to simplify invoice management, including data capture, approval workflows, reporting, and integration with other financial systems.

1. **Automated Data Capture**:
   - Concur Invoice uses Optical Character Recognition (OCR) to capture data from invoices automatically, extracting information such as invoice number, date, amount, and vendor details.
   - This feature reduces the need for manual data entry and ensures that invoices are accurately recorded.
2. **Customizable Approval Workflows**:
   - Concur Invoice allows organizations to set up approval workflows based on criteria such as invoice amount, department, or vendor.

- These workflows ensure that invoices are reviewed and approved by the right people, helping enforce compliance with company policies.

3. **Invoice Matching**:
   - The system can match invoices with purchase orders and receipts to verify that the billed amounts align with agreed-upon terms and received goods or services.
   - Matching helps prevent overpayments and ensures that invoices reflect actual purchases.

4. **Real-Time Reporting**:
   - Concur Invoice provides real-time reporting on invoice status, spend by vendor, approval times, and other metrics.
   - These insights help organizations make data-driven decisions, optimize vendor relationships, and monitor spending.

5. **Seamless Integration**:
   - Concur Invoice integrates with various ERP systems, such as SAP and Oracle, allowing seamless data transfer between accounts payable and other financial systems.
   - Integration reduces data duplication and supports a single source of truth for financial data.

Step 1: Setting Up Concur Invoice

Setting up Concur Invoice involves configuring invoice settings, creating workflows, and integrating with your ERP or financial systems. Proper setup ensures a smooth invoice process tailored to your organization's needs.

1. **Configuring Basic Invoice Settings**:
    - Start by configuring the basic settings in Concur Invoice, including default currency, tax settings, and any custom fields your organization requires.
    - These settings provide a foundation for all invoices processed in the system, ensuring consistency and compliance with regional regulations.
2. **Setting Up Vendors and Purchase Orders**:
    - Add your vendors to Concur Invoice, including essential details such as vendor name, contact information, and payment terms.
    - For companies using purchase orders, configure settings to allow invoice matching with POs, making it easier to verify invoice accuracy.
3. **Customizing Approval Workflows**:
    - Define approval workflows based on your company's policies. For instance, invoices

over a certain amount may require multiple levels of approval.
   - o Workflows can be customized based on factors like department, region, or vendor, ensuring that invoices receive the appropriate level of review.
4. **Integrating with Financial Systems**:
   - o Integrate Concur Invoice with your ERP or financial system to enable data sharing between accounts payable and other financial records.
   - o Integration ensures that invoice data flows seamlessly from Concur Invoice to your financial system, reducing the need for manual data transfers.

Step 2: Capturing and Entering Invoices

Once Concur Invoice is set up, the next step is to capture and enter invoices into the system. Concur Invoice provides several options for invoice entry, including automatic capture, email import, and manual entry.

1. **Using OCR for Automatic Data Capture**:
   - o Concur Invoice's OCR technology reads invoice documents and automatically extracts information such as invoice number, date, amount, and vendor details.

- OCR reduces manual data entry and ensures that invoices are accurately recorded with minimal effort from accounts payable staff.

2. **Importing Invoices via Email**:
   - Vendors can email invoices directly to a designated email address (e.g., invoices@concur.com), where Concur Invoice automatically captures and processes them.
   - This method is convenient for digital invoices, as it ensures that invoices are promptly received and entered into the system.

3. **Manual Invoice Entry**:
   - For paper invoices or invoices that require specific handling, Concur Invoice offers manual entry options. Accounts payable staff can enter details directly into the system, ensuring accuracy.
   - Manual entry allows staff to capture custom fields or additional details not extracted through OCR.

4. **Organizing Invoices for Review**:
   - All captured and entered invoices appear in Concur Invoice's central dashboard, where accounts payable staff can view, sort, and prioritize invoices for review and approval.

Step 3: Managing Invoice Approval Workflows

Once invoices are captured, they are routed through the configured approval workflows, ensuring that each invoice is reviewed and approved according to company policies.

1. **Setting Approval Requirements**:
   - Define approval requirements based on criteria such as invoice amount, vendor, or department. For example, invoices over a certain threshold may require finance or senior management approval.
   - Clear approval requirements ensure compliance and reduce the risk of unauthorized payments.
2. **Reviewing and Approving Invoices**:
   - Approvers can review invoices directly within Concur Invoice, examining details such as vendor information, billed amount, and matching purchase orders.
   - Approvers can approve, reject, or request additional information, providing feedback directly in the system.
3. **Handling Rejections and Adjustments**:
   - If an invoice is rejected, Concur Invoice notifies the accounts payable team to take further action, such as clarifying details with the vendor or making necessary adjustments.

- This feature ensures that all invoices meet company standards before they reach the payment stage.
4. **Tracking Invoice Status**:
    - Concur Invoice provides real-time tracking for each invoice, showing statuses such as "Pending Approval," "Approved," or "Rejected."
    - Real-time tracking improves visibility into invoice progress, helping accounts payable manage outstanding invoices and identify bottlenecks.

Step 4: Matching Invoices with Purchase Orders

Matching invoices to purchase orders and receipts ensures accuracy, preventing overpayment and verifying that the organization only pays for goods or services received.

1. **Three-Way Matching**:
    - Three-way matching involves verifying that the invoice amount matches the purchase order and receipt records. This process helps ensure that billed amounts align with agreed-upon terms.
    - Concur Invoice flags discrepancies, prompting accounts payable staff to review and resolve differences before proceeding with approval.

2. **Setting Tolerance Levels**:
   - Organizations can set tolerance levels in Concur Invoice to allow minor discrepancies within acceptable limits. For example, a 2% tolerance on total costs might be allowed without triggering an audit.
   - Tolerance levels streamline processing by reducing the need for manual review of minor variations.
3. **Resolving Matching Discrepancies**:
   - If an invoice does not match the purchase order, Concur Invoice notifies the accounts payable team, allowing them to investigate and resolve the issue.
   - This feature ensures that only accurate invoices proceed to payment, improving cost control and vendor accountability.

Step 5: Processing and Paying Invoices

Once invoices are approved, Concur Invoice routes them for payment, integrating with your financial system to initiate payment and complete the process.

1. **Scheduling Payments**:
   - Approved invoices can be scheduled for payment based on vendor terms, ensuring timely payments while optimizing cash flow.

- o Concur Invoice provides options for scheduling payments, helping organizations manage cash flow more effectively and avoid late fees.
2. **Integrating with Accounts Payable**:
   - o Concur Invoice integrates seamlessly with accounts payable, allowing for automatic payment initiation in the organization's financial system.
   - o Integration reduces manual data transfers and provides a unified view of financial obligations.
3. **Tracking Payment Status**:
   - o After payment initiation, Concur Invoice tracks payment status, providing updates such as "Payment Initiated" or "Payment Complete."
   - o Real-time tracking of payment status ensures transparency and allows accounts payable teams to manage follow-ups with vendors when necessary.
4. **Archiving Invoices for Compliance and Auditing**:
   - o All paid invoices are archived in Concur Invoice's digital repository, ensuring that records are accessible for audits and compliance checks.
   - o Archived invoices are searchable by criteria such as vendor, date, or amount, simplifying record-keeping and supporting audit readiness.

Reporting and Analytics in Concur Invoice

Concur Invoice's reporting and analytics tools provide valuable insights into spending trends, vendor performance, and invoice processing times, helping organizations optimize their accounts payable operations.

1. **Tracking Invoice Processing Times**:
   - Reports on processing times help organizations identify bottlenecks in the approval workflow, enabling continuous improvement.
   - Faster processing times reduce delays and improve vendor relationships by ensuring timely payments.
2. **Analyzing Spending by Vendor**:
   - Concur Invoice's reporting tools allow organizations to track spending by vendor, helping assess vendor performance and negotiate better terms.
   - Vendor-specific insights support data-driven decision-making and improve procurement strategies.
3. **Monitoring Compliance with Invoice Policies**:
   - Compliance reports highlight any invoices that failed to meet policy requirements, providing visibility into potential areas of risk.

- Monitoring compliance helps organizations maintain control over expenses and align with audit and regulatory standards.

4. **Using Predictive Analytics for Cash Flow Management**:
   - Predictive analytics in Concur Invoice forecast future cash flow needs based on current invoice data, enabling proactive financial planning.
   - Cash flow insights help organizations plan payments strategically, ensuring that funds are available when needed.

Best Practices for Managing Concur Invoice

To maximize the benefits of Concur Invoice, follow these best practices:

1. **Encourage Vendors to Send Digital Invoices**:
   - Request that vendors send invoices via email to facilitate automatic capture and reduce the need for manual entry.
   - Digital invoices streamline processing and improve accuracy in data capture.

2. **Regularly Review and Update Approval Workflows**:
   - Ensure that approval workflows align with current business needs and

compliance standards by regularly reviewing and updating them.
- o Updated workflows improve efficiency and ensure that invoices receive appropriate oversight.

3. **Monitor Invoice Processing Metrics**:
   - o Track metrics such as average processing time, policy compliance, and matching discrepancies to identify areas for improvement.
   - o Monitoring metrics helps organizations continuously improve invoice processing efficiency.

4. **Implement Vendor Communication Protocols**:
   - o Establish protocols for communicating with vendors regarding invoice discrepancies, payment status, and processing times.
   - o Clear communication improves vendor relationships and ensures smooth invoice management.

Conclusion

Concur Invoice provides organizations with an efficient, automated solution for managing the invoice lifecycle, from data capture to approval and payment. By using Concur Invoice's tools for data capture, matching, and workflow automation, companies can reduce processing times, improve compliance, and gain valuable insights into their spending.

In the next chapter, we'll explore **Setting Up Invoice Workflows**.

This chapter introduces Concur Invoice and provides a comprehensive overview of its features and processes.

Chapter 15: Setting Up Invoice Workflows

Introduction

Setting up invoice workflows in Concur Invoice is essential for streamlining the approval process, ensuring policy compliance, and managing invoices efficiently. Properly configured workflows enable organizations to automate approvals based on criteria such as invoice amount, department, and vendor, reducing processing times and minimizing errors. In this chapter, we will explore the steps to set up invoice workflows, from defining approval criteria to managing exceptions and fine-tuning the process for optimal efficiency.

The Importance of Invoice Workflows

Effective invoice workflows offer several benefits for organizations, including:

1. **Improved Efficiency**: Automated workflows reduce manual intervention, speeding up the approval process and freeing up staff for higher-value tasks.
2. **Enhanced Compliance**: Workflows ensure that invoices meet policy requirements, helping organizations enforce spending limits, vendor approvals, and other criteria.

3. **Reduced Errors**: Automation reduces human errors, such as misrouted invoices or missed approvals, improving accuracy in accounts payable.
4. **Increased Visibility**: Real-time tracking in Concur Invoice provides insight into the status of each invoice, helping accounts payable teams manage outstanding payments and identify bottlenecks.

Key Elements of an Invoice Workflow in Concur Invoice

An effective workflow in Concur Invoice consists of several key components that ensure each invoice follows the proper path for review and approval:

1. **Approval Criteria**: Criteria based on factors such as invoice amount, vendor, department, and spending category determine the workflow for each invoice.
2. **Approval Levels**: Different levels of approval are assigned based on the complexity or value of the invoice, such as requiring higher-level approval for larger amounts.
3. **Automated Policy Checks**: Built-in checks flag any policy violations, helping approvers address non-compliant items before approval.
4. **Exception Handling**: The workflow includes steps for managing exceptions, such as expedited approvals for urgent invoices or handling out-of-policy expenses.

Step 1: Defining Approval Criteria for Workflows

The first step in setting up an invoice workflow is to define the criteria that will determine the path each invoice follows. Approval criteria vary based on organizational policies and can include invoice amount, vendor, department, and more.

1. **Setting Up Approval Based on Invoice Amount**:
   - Establish different approval levels based on the invoice amount. For example, invoices under $1,000 may require a single approval, while those over $10,000 require multiple levels.
   - Amount-based approval helps ensure that high-value invoices receive the appropriate level of review, providing extra oversight for significant expenses.
2. **Defining Department-Specific Approval**:
   - Configure department-based approval to route invoices to the relevant department manager or head. For example, marketing invoices go to the marketing manager, while IT-related invoices go to the IT department head.
   - Department-specific workflows improve accountability and ensure that the correct approver reviews each invoice.

3. **Establishing Vendor-Specific Approval Rules**:
   - Set up vendor-based approval rules for specific vendors with unique terms or contracts. For instance, high-volume vendors may require finance department approval.
   - Vendor-based criteria help enforce vendor agreements and ensure consistent handling of vendor-related expenses.
4. **Customizing Approval for Different Expense Types**:
   - Create workflows based on expense type or category, such as travel, office supplies, or consulting services. Expense-specific workflows ensure that invoices align with category-specific policies.
   - Expense-type criteria allow for specialized handling of certain expenses, such as additional review for travel or consulting invoices.

Step 2: Configuring Approval Levels in Concur Invoice

Approval levels ensure that invoices receive the necessary review based on complexity, amount, or category. In Concur Invoice, you can configure multiple levels of approval to add layers of oversight.

1. **Defining Single vs. Multi-Level Approval**:
   - For lower-value or routine invoices, configure single-level approval, where one approver can authorize the payment.
   - For high-value or complex invoices, configure multi-level approval, requiring multiple approvers from different departments or authority levels.
2. **Assigning Role-Based Approval**:
   - Assign roles such as department head, finance director, or senior executive as approvers based on the level of oversight needed.
   - Role-based approval ensures that appropriate individuals are responsible for authorizing expenses within their scope.
3. **Setting Up Conditional Approvals for High-Risk Invoices**:
   - Define conditions that trigger additional approval for high-risk invoices, such as those with policy violations, unusual vendors, or high-dollar amounts.
   - Conditional approvals provide extra scrutiny for invoices with higher risk, helping reduce potential compliance issues.
4. **Defining Limits for Automatic Approval**:
   - Configure automatic approval thresholds for low-value invoices that do not require

detailed review, such as routine office supplies under $50.

- o Automatic approvals reduce manual workload by processing low-risk invoices quickly, allowing approvers to focus on higher-value items.

Step 3: Automating Policy Compliance Checks

Automated policy compliance checks are a critical part of Concur Invoice workflows, helping identify issues such as policy violations, missing documentation, or duplicate invoices.

1. **Setting Up Policy Rules**:
   - o Configure policy rules that align with organizational guidelines, such as spending limits, receipt requirements, and preferred vendor use.
   - o Policy rules automatically flag items that deviate from these guidelines, ensuring consistent enforcement of company policies.
2. **Flagging Out-of-Policy Invoices**:
   - o Use Concur Invoice's automated checks to flag invoices that do not comply with policy, such as those exceeding category limits or using non-preferred vendors.
   - o Flagged items prompt approvers to review details before proceeding,

reducing the risk of unauthorized payments.

3. **Identifying Duplicate Invoices**:
   - Set up Concur Invoice to detect duplicate invoices based on criteria such as invoice number, amount, and date. Duplicates are flagged for review to prevent double payments.
   - Duplicate detection helps maintain data integrity and prevent overpayment, supporting accurate accounts payable records.

4. **Ensuring Documentation Completeness**:
   - Policy rules can require certain fields or attachments, such as a purchase order (PO) or vendor contract. Missing documentation is flagged, ensuring that all invoices meet minimum requirements before approval.
   - This feature reduces follow-ups and minimizes the risk of processing incomplete invoices.

Step 4: Managing Workflow Exceptions

Occasionally, invoices require exception handling due to urgent payment needs, missing documentation, or out-of-policy expenses. Setting up exception handling ensures these invoices are processed correctly without disrupting compliance.

1. **Defining Expedited Approval for Urgent Invoices**:
   - Create a fast-track approval path for invoices marked as urgent, ensuring that critical payments, such as utility bills, are not delayed.
   - Expedited approval paths help prevent late fees or service disruptions, maintaining continuity in essential services.

2. **Allowing Conditional Approval for Policy Exceptions**:
   - Enable conditional approval for invoices that fall outside policy limits but have a valid justification, such as emergency purchases or vendor price changes.
   - Conditional approval workflows give approvers flexibility to address exceptions without compromising compliance.

3. **Setting Up Escalation Paths for Delayed Approvals**:
   - Define escalation paths for invoices that remain unapproved past a specified timeframe, such as forwarding the invoice to a higher-level approver if initial approval is delayed.
   - Escalation paths prevent bottlenecks and ensure timely processing of invoices,

supporting efficient accounts payable management.

4. **Implementing Hold and Review for Suspicious Invoices**:
    - Configure workflows to place certain invoices on hold for additional review, such as those flagged by audit or identified as potential fraud risks.
    - Hold and review steps add an extra layer of protection, allowing for careful examination before approval or rejection.

Step 5: Testing and Fine-Tuning Invoice Workflows

Once workflows are configured, it's important to test them thoroughly and fine-tune the setup for maximum efficiency. Testing ensures that workflows function as expected and that all approval paths are properly configured.

1. **Conducting Workflow Tests**:
    - Test each workflow with sample invoices that match different criteria, such as low-value, high-value, and out-of-policy invoices.
    - Testing verifies that invoices route correctly, ensuring that approvals follow the intended workflow paths.

2. **Reviewing Approval Times and Bottlenecks**:
   - Monitor approval times to identify any delays or bottlenecks, particularly for multi-level or high-value workflows.
   - Addressing bottlenecks improves efficiency and ensures that invoices are processed within target timelines.
3. **Collecting Feedback from Approvers**:
   - Gather feedback from approvers to identify potential issues, such as unnecessary steps or unclear approval criteria.
   - Feedback from users provides insights that can help refine workflows and improve usability.
4. **Making Adjustments Based on Analytics**:
   - Use analytics in Concur Invoice to assess workflow performance, including approval times, policy compliance rates, and exception handling frequency.
   - Analytics help identify areas for improvement, allowing organizations to optimize workflows based on real-world data.

Best Practices for Setting Up Invoice Workflows

Following best practices ensures that your invoice workflows in Concur Invoice are efficient, compliant, and aligned with organizational needs.

1. **Customize Workflows to Align with Policies**:
   o Ensure that workflows reflect your organization's policies on spending limits, vendor approvals, and documentation requirements.
   o Customization supports compliance and ensures that workflows meet company standards for invoice processing.
2. **Maintain Flexibility for Special Cases**:
   o While workflows should enforce policies, maintain flexibility for special cases such as emergency expenses or unique vendor terms.
   o Flexible workflows reduce the need for manual intervention while addressing exceptions effectively.
3. **Automate Low-Risk Invoices for Efficiency**:
   o Use automated approval thresholds for low-risk invoices, such as routine office supplies under a certain dollar amount.
   o Automation for low-risk items allows staff to focus on higher-value invoices that require more attention.
4. **Monitor Workflow Performance Regularly**:
   o Regularly review workflow performance to identify areas for improvement, such as delays, frequent exceptions, or common policy violations.

- Monitoring performance ensures that workflows remain efficient and responsive to business needs.

5. **Involve Key Stakeholders in Workflow Design**:
   - Collaborate with finance, procurement, and department heads when setting up workflows to ensure alignment with organizational needs.
   - Stakeholder input improves workflow design, creating a system that works effectively for all departments involved in invoice processing.

Common Issues and Troubleshooting in Invoice Workflows

While Concur Invoice's workflows are designed to be efficient, occasional issues may arise. Here's how to address common challenges.

1. **Incorrect Routing of Invoices**:
   - If invoices are routed incorrectly, review the workflow criteria to ensure they are set up correctly. Verify that criteria match the intended conditions for each path.
   - Correcting routing criteria ensures that invoices are directed to the appropriate approvers.

2. **Approval Delays**:
    - Approval delays can occur due to unclear roles or a backlog with specific approvers. Consider adding additional approvers or setting up escalation paths for high-priority invoices.
    - Escalation paths ensure that delays are managed and that invoices do not remain unapproved for extended periods.
3. **Frequent Policy Violations**:
    - If policy violations are common, review the policy rules to ensure they align with current business needs. Consider updating spending limits or preferred vendor lists.
    - Updating policies based on workflow data helps reduce violations and improves compliance.
4. **Workflow Configuration Errors**:
    - Errors in workflow configuration may prevent workflows from functioning correctly. Review settings, test workflows, and consult Concur Invoice support if issues persist.
    - Regular testing and validation help ensure that workflows operate smoothly.

Conclusion

Setting up invoice workflows in Concur Invoice is essential for efficient, accurate, and compliant invoice processing. By defining approval criteria, configuring multi-level approvals, automating compliance checks, and managing exceptions, organizations can streamline the invoice lifecycle and improve control over spending.

In the next chapter, we'll explore **Capturing Invoices and Vendor Management**.

This chapter provides a comprehensive guide to setting up effective invoice workflows in Concur Invoice.

Chapter 16: Capturing Invoices and Vendor Management

Introduction

Capturing invoices and managing vendor relationships effectively are critical to streamlining accounts payable operations in SAP Concur. Efficient invoice capture ensures that all invoices are processed accurately and on time, while effective vendor management strengthens partnerships, enhances compliance, and improves negotiation capabilities. This chapter will cover methods for capturing invoices in Concur Invoice, best practices for data accuracy, and strategies for effective vendor management.

The Importance of Accurate Invoice Capture and Vendor Management

Proper invoice capture and vendor management offer several benefits to organizations, including:

1. **Reduced Processing Time**: Efficient capture of invoices minimizes delays, improving the overall speed of the accounts payable process.
2. **Increased Data Accuracy**: Automated capture and validation reduce the risk of errors, ensuring that vendor invoices are accurately recorded.
3. **Improved Vendor Relationships**: Good vendor management practices promote positive

partnerships and enable better negotiation of terms.

4. **Enhanced Compliance**: Accurate invoice capture and proper vendor information ensure that organizations meet regulatory and policy standards, supporting audit readiness.

Methods for Capturing Invoices in Concur Invoice

Concur Invoice offers various methods for capturing invoices, including automated data capture, email import, and manual entry. These options provide flexibility and enable organizations to process invoices from multiple sources efficiently.

1. **Automatic Data Capture Using OCR**:
   - Concur Invoice's Optical Character Recognition (OCR) technology automates data capture by scanning and extracting information from invoices. Key details, such as invoice number, vendor name, date, and amount, are recorded automatically.
   - OCR significantly reduces manual data entry, ensuring accurate capture and quick processing of invoices.
2. **Importing Invoices via Email**:
   - Vendors can send invoices directly to a designated email address (e.g., invoices@concur.com). Concur Invoice

captures the invoices from the email, allowing them to enter the processing workflow immediately.

- o Email imports are ideal for digital invoices, reducing manual handling and enabling timely entry into the accounts payable system.

3. **Capturing Invoices via the Concur Mobile App**:
    - o The Concur mobile app allows accounts payable staff to capture paper invoices on the go by taking a photo with a smartphone. OCR processes the image and extracts relevant information, populating fields automatically.
    - o Mobile capture is useful for remote or field staff, enabling them to enter invoices promptly, regardless of location.

4. **Manual Invoice Entry for Specific Cases**:
    - o For invoices that may not meet standard criteria or require specific handling, accounts payable staff can manually enter invoice details in Concur Invoice.
    - o Manual entry allows staff to customize entries, ensuring that invoices with special terms or conditions are captured accurately.

Step 1: Configuring OCR for Accurate Data Capture

OCR technology is integral to efficient invoice capture in Concur Invoice. Configuring OCR settings ensures optimal performance, accuracy, and consistent data extraction from invoices.

1. **Setting Up OCR Parameters**:
   - Define the fields for OCR to capture, such as invoice number, amount, vendor name, and date. Ensure these fields align with the organization's data requirements.
   - By customizing OCR parameters, organizations can improve data extraction accuracy and reduce the need for manual corrections.
2. **Establishing Quality Standards for Scanned Invoices**:
   - Ensure that scanned images are clear and legible, as OCR accuracy relies on image quality. Establish standards for resolution, brightness, and alignment to maintain data capture integrity.
   - Quality standards for scanned invoices minimize errors in OCR processing and improve the speed of invoice entry.
3. **Reviewing and Validating OCR-Extracted Data**:
   - Regularly review OCR-captured data for accuracy, particularly for new vendor

formats or unusual invoice layouts. Validation helps identify potential issues early.

o Routine validation maintains data integrity and minimizes discrepancies in the accounts payable process.

4. **Training Staff on Best Practices for OCR Capture**:

o Train accounts payable staff on using OCR and recognizing limitations. Staff should know how to handle exceptions, such as unclear images or unique invoice formats.

o Training ensures that staff members are equipped to manage OCR effectively, reducing errors and optimizing data capture.

Step 2: Importing and Organizing Invoices from Email

Email imports simplify the invoice capture process, particularly for vendors who send digital invoices. Organizing the email import process ensures that invoices are received, processed, and recorded efficiently.

1. **Setting Up a Dedicated Invoice Email Address**:

o Create a dedicated email address for receiving vendor invoices, such as invoices@concur.com, which Concur Invoice can monitor automatically.

- A dedicated email address centralizes invoice submission, making it easier to manage incoming invoices and ensuring they are entered promptly.

2. **Training Vendors on Email Submission Guidelines**:
    - Provide vendors with submission guidelines, including acceptable formats (e.g., PDF), required details, and the designated email address.
    - Clear guidelines improve the quality and consistency of email submissions, minimizing delays in processing invoices.

3. **Organizing Incoming Invoices for Processing**:
    - Concur Invoice organizes incoming invoices in a central dashboard, where accounts payable staff can view, sort, and prioritize them based on urgency or other criteria.
    - Central organization reduces clutter and ensures that high-priority invoices receive immediate attention.

4. **Automating Acknowledgements for Received Invoices**:
    - Set up automated acknowledgments to confirm receipt of invoices, providing vendors with assurance that their

invoices have been received and are in the processing queue.
  - o Automated responses improve vendor communication and reduce follow-up inquiries, streamlining the invoice submission process.

Step 3: Managing Vendor Information and Relationships

Vendor management in Concur Invoice involves maintaining accurate records for each vendor and establishing processes that support efficient, compliant invoicing.

1. **Creating and Updating Vendor Profiles**:
   - o Set up a profile for each vendor with essential details, including contact information, payment terms, tax identification, and preferred currency.
   - o Accurate vendor profiles improve efficiency by ensuring that invoices are processed according to vendor-specific requirements, reducing manual adjustments.
2. **Assigning Preferred Vendors**:
   - o Designate preferred vendors within Concur Invoice to prioritize their invoices and support compliance with procurement policies.

- Preferred vendors often offer better terms or discounts, and prioritizing them ensures that organizations maximize these benefits.
3. **Setting Payment Terms and Conditions**:
   - Define payment terms for each vendor, such as net 30 or net 60, and include any specific conditions or discounts for early payment.
   - Clear payment terms support timely processing and help organizations take advantage of early payment discounts, optimizing cash flow.
4. **Tracking Vendor Performance Metrics**:
   - Use Concur Invoice's reporting tools to monitor vendor performance, tracking metrics such as on-time delivery, quality, and dispute frequency.
   - Tracking performance metrics informs vendor relationship management, helping organizations identify top-performing vendors and address issues with underperforming ones.

Step 4: Implementing Compliance Checks for Vendor Invoices

Compliance checks in Concur Invoice ensure that all vendor invoices meet regulatory, policy, and documentation requirements before approval, supporting audit readiness.

1. **Configuring Compliance Rules**:
   - Set up compliance rules to verify each invoice's alignment with company policies, such as allowable expense categories, maximum amounts, and required documentation.
   - Compliance rules automate the review process, ensuring that invoices meet standards before they enter the approval workflow.

2. **Verifying Required Documentation**:
   - Require vendors to provide necessary documentation, such as purchase orders (POs) or delivery receipts, to accompany invoices.
   - Document verification reduces the risk of fraudulent or erroneous invoices and ensures that each invoice reflects a legitimate transaction.

3. **Flagging Out-of-Policy Invoices**:
   - Use automated flags to identify invoices that do not meet policy criteria, such as those from non-preferred vendors or those exceeding specified limits.
   - Flagged invoices receive additional scrutiny, helping prevent unauthorized

payments and supporting policy compliance.

4. **Establishing Vendor Compliance Reviews**:
   - Conduct periodic reviews of vendor compliance, assessing whether vendors adhere to agreed-upon terms and conditions, such as providing accurate invoices and timely submissions.
   - Vendor compliance reviews strengthen partnerships and help organizations maintain a high standard of invoice quality.

Step 5: Monitoring and Analyzing Invoice and Vendor Data

Concur Invoice's reporting and analytics tools provide insights into invoice processing and vendor performance, helping organizations optimize accounts payable operations.

1. **Tracking Invoice Processing Times**:
   - Use Concur Invoice's analytics to monitor processing times for each invoice, from capture to payment approval, identifying bottlenecks or delays.
   - Reducing processing times improves efficiency, ensuring that vendors are paid on time and accounts payable operates smoothly.

2. **Analyzing Spending by Vendor**:
   - Generate reports to track spending by vendor, providing visibility into procurement costs and identifying opportunities for negotiation or consolidation.
   - Spending insights support data-driven decision-making and improve procurement strategies.
3. **Assessing Vendor Compliance and Reliability**:
   - Review compliance rates and reliability metrics, such as on-time delivery and invoice accuracy, to evaluate vendor performance.
   - Reliable vendor data helps organizations make informed choices about vendor partnerships and negotiate better terms.
4. **Forecasting Cash Flow and Budgeting**:
   - Concur Invoice's predictive analytics help forecast future cash flow based on current invoice data, supporting proactive budgeting and financial planning.
   - Accurate cash flow forecasting enables better planning for expenses and helps ensure that funds are available for upcoming payments.

Best Practices for Capturing Invoices and Managing Vendors

Following best practices for capturing invoices and managing vendors ensures that your accounts payable process is efficient, compliant, and aligned with organizational goals.

1. **Encourage Vendors to Submit Digital Invoices**:
   - Digital invoices streamline processing and reduce the need for manual entry. Encourage vendors to use email submissions to minimize delays.
   - Digital submission improves efficiency and supports faster invoice processing.
2. **Regularly Update Vendor Information**:
   - Keep vendor profiles current by regularly updating contact information, payment terms, and other relevant details. Up-to-date information prevents errors and facilitates smooth invoice processing.
   - Regular updates ensure accuracy and help maintain strong vendor relationships.
3. **Use Automated Data Capture Whenever Possible**:
   - Leverage OCR and automated email capture for invoice entry, minimizing manual data handling and improving data accuracy.

- o Automation reduces errors, saves time, and enhances overall process efficiency.
4. **Maintain Clear Communication with Vendors**:
   - o Set clear expectations with vendors regarding invoice submission guidelines, payment terms, and compliance requirements.
   - o Open communication fosters positive vendor relationships and ensures that both parties understand and meet expectations.
5. **Monitor Compliance and Performance Metrics Regularly**:
   - o Track metrics for vendor compliance, invoice processing times, and spending trends to assess performance and identify improvement areas.
   - o Regular monitoring helps optimize accounts payable processes and informs strategic decision-making.

Common Issues and Troubleshooting in Invoice Capture and Vendor Management

While Concur Invoice is designed to simplify invoice capture and vendor management, occasional issues may arise. Here's how to address some common challenges.

1. **Low OCR Accuracy for Certain Invoices**:
   - o If OCR accuracy is low for specific invoices, ensure that image quality meets recommended standards. Alternatively, adjust OCR settings for better results.
   - o Improving image quality or adjusting settings helps optimize OCR performance.
2. **Delayed Invoice Processing**:
   - o Delays can occur if invoices are not submitted on time or lack required documentation. Ensure vendors understand submission timelines and requirements.
   - o Clear guidelines and reminders reduce delays and improve processing times.
3. **Incomplete or Incorrect Vendor Profiles**:
   - o Incomplete profiles can lead to processing errors. Regularly review and update vendor information to ensure that profiles contain all necessary details.
   - o Accurate profiles support efficient invoice handling and reduce processing issues.
4. **Frequent Policy Violations**:
   - o If certain vendors frequently submit out-of-policy invoices, consider providing additional guidance on compliance or reviewing policy requirements.

o   Addressing recurring issues with vendors
      helps maintain consistent compliance.

Conclusion

Efficient invoice capture and effective vendor management are essential to optimizing accounts payable processes. By leveraging SAP Concur's tools for data capture, vendor profiles, and compliance checks, organizations can improve invoice accuracy, maintain strong vendor relationships, and support strategic financial management.

In the next chapter, we will explore advanced approval workflows, focusing on best practices for handling complex approvals and ensuring policy adherence throughout the invoice lifecycle.

This chapter provides a detailed guide to capturing invoices and managing vendors in Concur Invoice.

Chapter 17: Integrating SAP Concur with ERP Systems

Introduction

Integrating SAP Concur with an ERP (Enterprise Resource Planning) system enables seamless data flow between expense management and broader financial operations, creating a unified platform for managing expenses, invoices, and vendor payments. This integration streamlines accounts payable workflows, enhances data accuracy, and provides real-time visibility into financial data across systems. In this chapter, we will explore the importance of ERP integration, the steps to set up integration with SAP Concur, and best practices for ensuring smooth and efficient data exchange.

The Importance of ERP Integration with SAP Concur

Integrating SAP Concur with an ERP system offers several key benefits, including:

1. **Enhanced Data Accuracy**: Integration reduces manual data entry and automates data transfer, minimizing the risk of errors and ensuring accurate financial reporting.
2. **Improved Visibility**: Real-time data exchange between SAP Concur and the ERP system provides comprehensive visibility into expenses,

vendor payments, and cash flow, enabling better financial decision-making.

3. **Increased Efficiency**: By automating data flow, integration reduces redundancy, eliminates double entry, and streamlines workflows, saving time for finance and accounts payable teams.

4. **Stronger Compliance and Audit Readiness**: A unified financial platform improves compliance tracking and simplifies auditing, as all expense and payment data is stored and organized in a centralized system.

Key Components of SAP Concur and ERP Integration

Successful integration between SAP Concur and an ERP system requires the alignment of several components to ensure seamless data flow and interoperability.

1. **Data Mapping**: Establishing mappings between fields in SAP Concur and corresponding fields in the ERP system, such as vendor details, invoice numbers, amounts, and GL (General Ledger) codes.

2. **Data Transfer Protocols**: Determining how data will move between SAP Concur and the ERP system, using methods like APIs (Application Programming Interfaces), middleware, or file transfers.

3. **Synchronization Frequency**: Setting up the frequency of data syncs, which may vary from

real-time updates to daily or weekly batch processing based on organizational needs.

4. **Error Handling and Notifications**: Implementing processes for handling errors in data transfer, such as notifications to alert administrators to incomplete or failed data syncs.

Step 1: Preparing for ERP Integration with SAP Concur

Preparing for integration involves reviewing organizational requirements, defining integration goals, and ensuring both systems are ready for data exchange.

1. **Identifying Integration Goals**:
   - Define the primary objectives for the integration, such as reducing data entry time, improving data accuracy, or achieving real-time expense tracking.
   - Clear goals help guide the integration setup and ensure that the solution meets business requirements.
2. **Reviewing Current Data Processes**:
   - Assess the current process for handling expense data and payments, identifying areas for improvement and noting any existing challenges in data handling between SAP Concur and the ERP system.
   - Understanding current processes allows for smoother integration planning and

highlights areas that may benefit from automation.

3. **Establishing Data Standards**:
   - Set data standards for fields that will be exchanged between SAP Concur and the ERP system, including vendor names, amounts, dates, and GL codes.
   - Consistent data standards reduce errors in integration and ensure that both systems interpret data in the same way.

4. **Collaborating with IT and Finance Teams**:
   - Work closely with IT and finance teams to plan the integration, as their expertise is essential for configuring technical settings, mapping data, and setting up workflows.
   - Collaboration ensures that the integration aligns with organizational policies and that all stakeholders are prepared for the transition.

Step 2: Setting Up Data Mapping Between SAP Concur and the ERP System

Data mapping is a crucial step that links fields in SAP Concur with corresponding fields in the ERP system, ensuring accurate and consistent data transfer.

1. **Mapping Core Fields**:
   o   Map core fields such as invoice number, vendor ID, date, amount, currency, and GL account codes between SAP Concur and the ERP system.
   o   Accurate mapping ensures that key data flows correctly, supporting accurate financial reporting and auditing.

2. **Handling Custom Fields**:
   o   For organizations that use custom fields in SAP Concur, map these fields to relevant fields in the ERP system. Examples might include cost center, department code, or project code.
   o   Mapping custom fields enables more detailed financial tracking and supports customized reporting in the ERP system.

3. **Setting Up Multi-Currency Mapping**:
   o   For global organizations, set up multi-currency mapping to ensure that amounts are recorded accurately, and exchange rates are consistent between systems.
   o   Multi-currency support enables accurate reporting across regions and supports consolidated financial analysis.

4. **Testing and Validating Data Mapping**:
   o   Test the data mapping to verify that each field transfers correctly. Validation helps

identify discrepancies or errors in mapping before full-scale deployment.
- o Conducting multiple test cycles ensures reliable data transfer and reduces the risk of errors once integration is live.

Step 3: Configuring Data Transfer Protocols

Data transfer protocols define how information flows between SAP Concur and the ERP system. Choosing the right protocol is essential for efficient data synchronization.

1. **Using APIs for Real-Time Data Transfer**:
   - o APIs provide a direct link between SAP Concur and the ERP system, allowing real-time data updates. APIs are ideal for organizations that need up-to-the-minute visibility into expenses and payments.
   - o Real-time integration with APIs ensures that changes in SAP Concur immediately reflect in the ERP, providing accurate, current financial data.
2. **Utilizing Middleware for Enhanced Data Management**:
   - o Middleware solutions act as intermediaries between SAP Concur and the ERP, facilitating data exchange, handling transformations, and providing additional data processing capabilities.

- Middleware is beneficial for complex integrations, as it can manage data transformation, error handling, and logging more efficiently.

3. **Setting Up File-Based Transfers for Batch Processing**:
   - For organizations that do not require real-time updates, file-based transfers offer an alternative by sending data batches at scheduled intervals (e.g., daily or weekly).
   - Batch processing reduces integration complexity and is suitable for smaller organizations or those with limited data transfer requirements.

4. **Configuring Secure Data Transfer**:
   - Ensure that all data transfers between SAP Concur and the ERP system use secure protocols, such as HTTPS or secure file transfer protocols (SFTP), to protect sensitive financial information.
   - Secure transfer protocols reduce data breach risks, ensuring compliance with regulatory standards for data privacy and security.

Step 4: Defining Data Sync Frequency and Timing

Determining the frequency and timing of data syncs allows organizations to balance data accuracy and processing efficiency based on their operational needs.

1. **Setting Real-Time Syncs for High-Volume Organizations**:
    - For organizations with high volumes of expenses and invoices, real-time syncs may be necessary to maintain up-to-date records.
    - Real-time syncs provide immediate visibility into expense data, improving cash flow management and enabling timely decision-making.
2. **Using Scheduled Syncs for Routine Updates**:
    - Scheduled syncs, such as daily or weekly updates, are sufficient for organizations with lower transaction volumes or those that do not require immediate data updates.
    - Routine updates reduce system load, providing accurate data while minimizing processing demands.
3. **Prioritizing Sync Timing to Minimize Disruption**:
    - Schedule data syncs during off-peak hours to reduce disruption and ensure that accounts payable and finance teams

have access to the latest data during regular working hours.

- Timing syncs effectively minimizes impact on day-to-day operations and improves overall system performance.

4. **Configuring Notifications for Sync Success and Failure**:
   - Set up notifications to alert administrators if data syncs are successful or if any errors occur. Notifications enable quick resolution of issues, minimizing data discrepancies.
   - Proactive error handling ensures that integration issues are resolved promptly, maintaining data integrity across systems.

Step 5: Handling Data Validation and Error Management

Error management ensures data integrity by identifying, tracking, and resolving any issues in data transfer between SAP Concur and the ERP system.

1. **Implementing Data Validation Checks**:
   - Set up validation checks for key data points, such as amounts, GL codes, and vendor IDs, to ensure data accuracy before transfer.

- o Validation checks catch discrepancies early, allowing corrections before data reaches the ERP system.
2. **Setting Up Error Logs and Tracking**:
   - o Configure error logging to track issues in data transfer, such as incomplete records or mismatched fields, making it easier to identify and resolve issues.
   - o Error logs provide visibility into recurring problems, enabling organizations to address root causes and improve integration reliability.
3. **Creating a Resolution Workflow for Data Errors**:
   - o Define a workflow for resolving errors, such as notifying specific team members and assigning responsibility for corrections.
   - o A clear resolution process ensures that data errors are resolved efficiently, maintaining data quality across systems.
4. **Establishing Escalation Protocols for Critical Errors**:
   - o For critical errors that disrupt integration or affect financial data accuracy, set up escalation protocols to alert management or IT for immediate resolution.
   - o Escalation protocols ensure rapid response to high-priority issues,

minimizing impact on financial reporting and compliance.

Monitoring and Optimizing ERP Integration

Once integration is live, ongoing monitoring and optimization ensure that data flows smoothly and that both systems perform effectively.

1. **Tracking Integration Performance Metrics**:
   - Monitor metrics such as data transfer speed, error rates, and sync frequency to assess integration performance and identify areas for improvement.
   - Tracking performance metrics allows organizations to optimize integration settings and maintain efficient data flow.
2. **Conducting Regular Data Reconciliation**:
   - Periodically reconcile data between SAP Concur and the ERP system to verify that records are consistent, addressing any discrepancies that may arise over time.
   - Regular reconciliation improves data accuracy and ensures alignment between both systems.
3. **Adjusting Sync Frequency Based on Data Needs**:
   - Based on operational needs, adjust sync frequency as necessary. For example, increase sync frequency during peak

expense periods to maintain accurate financial data.
- o Flexibility in sync timing allows organizations to adapt to changes in transaction volume and data requirements.

4. **Gathering Feedback from Finance and Accounts Payable Teams**:
   - o Collect feedback from finance and accounts payable staff on integration effectiveness, addressing any pain points and making improvements as needed.
   - o Employee feedback helps refine integration settings, ensuring that the solution supports day-to-day operations effectively.

Best Practices for Successful ERP Integration with SAP Concur

Following best practices during ERP integration with SAP Concur enhances data accuracy, improves workflow efficiency, and supports long-term integration success.

1. **Establish Clear Data Ownership**:
   - o Define data ownership responsibilities, such as who is responsible for managing vendor data, GL codes, and expense categories.

- Clear data ownership ensures accountability and consistency across systems.

2. **Regularly Update ERP and SAP Concur Settings**:
   - Keep settings and configurations in both SAP Concur and the ERP system current, especially when policies or data requirements change.
   - Regular updates prevent integration issues and ensure alignment with organizational standards.

3. **Automate Routine Processes to Reduce Manual Intervention**:
   - Use automation wherever possible, such as setting up batch processing, automated notifications, and error-handling workflows.
   - Automation reduces the risk of human error, improves efficiency, and allows staff to focus on higher-value tasks.

4. **Document Integration Workflows and Troubleshooting Steps**:
   - Maintain documentation for integration workflows, data mappings, error-handling protocols, and troubleshooting steps.
   - Documentation supports ongoing maintenance and enables quick resolution of issues, especially for new team members.

5. **Conduct Periodic Audits of Data Accuracy**:
    - o Perform audits to verify data accuracy between SAP Concur and the ERP system, ensuring that records align and that the integration operates as intended.
    - o Regular audits support compliance and maintain data integrity, strengthening financial reporting and decision-making.

Common Issues and Troubleshooting in ERP Integration

While ERP integration with SAP Concur streamlines workflows, some common challenges may arise. Here's how to address them effectively.

1. **Data Mismatch Errors**:
    - o If data mismatches occur, verify that mappings between fields are correct and that data standards are consistent across both systems.
    - o Addressing data mismatches ensures that information is accurately transferred and prevents discrepancies in financial reporting.
2. **Frequent Sync Failures**:
    - o Frequent failures may indicate network issues, configuration problems, or data volume limits. Work with IT to address

connectivity issues or adjust sync settings as necessary.

- o Troubleshooting sync failures improves reliability and minimizes disruptions in data flow.

3. **Inconsistent Multi-Currency Data**:
   - o For multi-currency organizations, inconsistencies may arise if exchange rates are not updated regularly. Ensure both systems use the same rates and update them as needed.
   - o Consistent exchange rates maintain accuracy in multi-currency transactions and prevent financial discrepancies.

4. **Slow Data Transfer Speeds**:
   - o Slow transfer speeds may result from network limitations or high data volumes. Consider batch processing or reviewing network settings to optimize transfer speed.
   - o Optimizing transfer settings reduces lag and ensures timely updates between systems.

Conclusion

Integrating SAP Concur with an ERP system enhances accounts payable efficiency, data accuracy, and financial visibility. By following this chapter's guidelines for setup, data mapping, error handling, and monitoring, organizations can create a unified financial platform that supports real-time insights and strategic decision-making.

In the next chapter, we'll explore advanced analytics and reporting in SAP Concur, focusing on how to use data insights to drive improvements in expense and invoice management.

This chapter provides a comprehensive guide to integrating SAP Concur with ERP systems.

Chapter 18: Invoice Reporting and Analytics

Introduction

Invoice reporting and analytics in SAP Concur provide powerful tools for organizations to gain insights into their accounts payable processes, monitor spending trends, and optimize vendor management. By leveraging data-driven insights, finance teams can make informed decisions, streamline workflows, and ensure compliance. This chapter explores the key reporting and analytics features in SAP Concur, covering essential reports, customization options, and best practices for analyzing invoice data to drive strategic improvements.

The Importance of Invoice Reporting and Analytics

Effective reporting and analytics for invoices enable organizations to achieve several strategic goals:

1. **Enhanced Financial Visibility**: Reports provide a comprehensive view of spending, allowing organizations to monitor cash flow and forecast financial needs accurately.
2. **Improved Vendor Management**: Tracking spending by vendor helps assess performance, manage relationships, and negotiate better terms.

3. **Compliance Monitoring**: Analytics identify policy violations, ensuring that invoices align with organizational standards and regulatory requirements.
4. **Increased Efficiency**: Analyzing processing times and approval workflows helps identify bottlenecks, streamline processes, and improve overall efficiency.

Key Reporting Features in SAP Concur

SAP Concur offers a variety of reporting and analytics tools that cater to different aspects of invoice management, allowing users to access detailed insights and track performance metrics.

1. **Standard Reports**:
   o SAP Concur includes a range of pre-built, standard reports covering essential metrics such as spend by vendor, invoice approval times, and policy compliance.
   o These reports provide quick access to critical data, allowing finance teams to monitor key performance indicators (KPIs) without the need for customization.
2. **Customizable Dashboards**:
   o Dashboards offer a visual overview of key metrics, such as total invoice spend, top vendors, and invoices pending approval.

Dashboards are customizable, enabling users to focus on the metrics most relevant to their roles.

- Customizable dashboards improve decision-making by highlighting priority data, helping users track performance at a glance.

3. **Ad Hoc Reporting**:
   - For organizations with specific reporting needs, SAP Concur's ad hoc reporting capabilities allow users to create custom reports based on unique criteria and data fields.
   - Ad hoc reports provide flexibility, enabling users to explore data in detail and answer specific questions that standard reports may not address.

4. **Data Export Options**:
   - SAP Concur offers export options for CSV, Excel, and PDF formats, allowing users to share reports or perform additional analysis in external tools.
   - Data exports support collaboration across departments and allow for integration with broader financial reporting processes.

Essential Invoice Reports in SAP Concur

SAP Concur's reporting suite includes several essential invoice reports that provide insights into spending, compliance, and workflow efficiency. Here are some key reports to leverage.

1. **Spend by Vendor Report**:
    o The Spend by Vendor report shows the total amount spent with each vendor over a specified period, helping organizations assess vendor performance and track spending trends.
    o By monitoring vendor spending, finance teams can identify top vendors, manage relationships, and negotiate favorable terms based on purchase volume.
2. **Invoice Processing Time Report**:
    o This report tracks the average time taken to process invoices, from submission to approval, providing insights into workflow efficiency.
    o Monitoring processing times allows organizations to identify bottlenecks, streamline workflows, and ensure timely payments to vendors.
3. **Policy Compliance Report**:
    o The Policy Compliance report highlights invoices that deviate from organizational policies, such as those exceeding

spending limits or lacking required documentation.

- ○ Compliance reports help enforce company policies, reduce non-compliance, and identify areas where additional training may be needed.

4. **Invoice Aging Report**:
   - ○ The Invoice Aging report categorizes invoices based on their age, such as 0-30 days, 31-60 days, and over 90 days. This report is critical for managing outstanding payments and tracking overdue invoices.
   - ○ Aging reports support cash flow management by identifying invoices that require immediate attention, ensuring timely payment to vendors and avoiding late fees.

5. **Approval Workflow Report**:
   - ○ This report provides insights into the performance of the approval workflow, showing metrics like average approval time, number of approvers per invoice, and any delays.
   - ○ Analyzing approval workflows helps organizations identify bottlenecks, optimize approval hierarchies, and reduce processing time.

6. **Top Expense Categories Report**:
    - o This report displays spending by category (e.g., travel, office supplies, consulting), helping organizations understand where most of their funds are allocated.
    - o Tracking expense categories allows finance teams to make data-driven decisions about budget allocation, cost-cutting measures, and policy adjustments.

Step 1: Setting Up and Customizing Reports

Setting up and customizing reports in SAP Concur ensures that organizations track the data most relevant to their financial goals and operational needs.

1. **Selecting Relevant Metrics**:
    - o Identify the metrics that align with organizational goals, such as processing speed, vendor spend, or compliance rates. Customize reports to include only the most relevant data.
    - o Focusing on key metrics provides a clear picture of performance, allowing finance teams to track progress and make informed decisions.
2. **Applying Filters for Specific Insights**:
    - o Use filters to narrow down data in reports, such as filtering by department,

time period, or invoice amount. Filters provide targeted insights, making it easier to analyze specific areas.
- o Filtering improves data analysis by focusing on particular aspects of performance, such as a department's compliance with spending limits or a vendor's processing time.

3. **Customizing Report Layouts and Views**:
   - o Customize report layouts to display data in a format that suits your team's preferences, such as charts, tables, or graphs. Arrange data fields in a way that highlights priority information.
   - o Tailored layouts make reports easier to interpret, supporting quick analysis and actionable insights.

4. **Scheduling Reports for Regular Distribution**:
   - o Set up automated report schedules for regular distribution to stakeholders, such as weekly or monthly reports on spending, compliance, or processing times.
   - o Scheduled reports keep stakeholders informed, reduce the need for manual reporting, and ensure timely access to key metrics.

Step 2: Analyzing Invoice Data for Insights

Effective analysis of invoice data helps organizations
make data-driven decisions that optimize expenses,
improve processes, and strengthen vendor
management.

1. **Identifying High-Value Vendors and Key Trends**:
    o   Review spend by vendor to identify top
        suppliers and assess whether spending
        aligns with expectations or presents
        opportunities for negotiation.
    o   High-value vendor analysis supports
        strategic sourcing decisions, helping
        organizations negotiate better terms
        with key vendors based on spending
        volume.
2. **Evaluating Processing Times for Bottlenecks**:
    o   Analyze invoice processing times to
        identify any bottlenecks, such as delays
        in specific approval stages or high-
        volume periods.
    o   Identifying bottlenecks allows finance
        teams to make process improvements,
        streamline workflows, and reduce overall
        processing time.
3. **Tracking Compliance Trends Over Time**:
    o   Use compliance reports to monitor
        trends in policy adherence, such as
        changes in the frequency of policy

violations or departments with recurrent non-compliance.

- o Analyzing compliance trends highlights areas where policies may need clarification or where additional training is required to improve adherence.

4. **Assessing Approval Workflow Efficiency**:
   - o Review the performance of approval workflows to determine whether the current process supports timely invoice approval. Identify whether approvals are consistently delayed by specific approvers or departments.
   - o Workflow analysis helps optimize the approval process, reducing delays and supporting timely vendor payments.

Step 3: Using Dashboards for Real-Time Tracking

Dashboards in SAP Concur provide a high-level view of essential metrics, allowing users to monitor real-time data and make quick adjustments as needed.

1. **Customizing Dashboard Widgets for Key Metrics**:
   - o Set up dashboard widgets to display critical metrics, such as total spend, invoices awaiting approval, and policy violations. Customization allows users to

prioritize data that requires immediate attention.

- o Personalized dashboards enable quick decision-making, as users can see essential information without navigating multiple reports.

2. **Tracking Pending Invoices and Approvals**:
   - o Use dashboards to monitor pending invoices, especially those nearing due dates or those pending approval. This real-time visibility ensures that critical invoices are processed promptly.
   - o Tracking pending invoices helps organizations avoid late fees and maintain positive vendor relationships by ensuring timely payments.

3. **Monitoring Spending Patterns by Category**:
   - o Track spending patterns by category, such as office supplies or travel, to identify shifts in spending behavior and adjust budgets accordingly.
   - o Monitoring spending categories provides insights into budget allocation, helping organizations manage expenses effectively.

4. **Setting Alerts for Out-of-Policy Invoices**:
   - o Configure alerts for out-of-policy invoices, notifying finance teams or managers when an invoice requires immediate attention.

- Alerts improve compliance by ensuring that policy deviations are addressed promptly, reducing the risk of unauthorized expenses.

Step 4: Exporting Data for Cross-Departmental Analysis

Data exports enable organizations to share invoice data with other departments, facilitating cross-departmental analysis and supporting broader financial planning.

1. **Exporting Reports in CSV, Excel, and PDF Formats:**
   - Use SAP Concur's export options to save reports in CSV, Excel, or PDF formats, allowing for easy sharing and further analysis in external tools.
   - Data exports support collaboration, allowing teams across departments to access and analyze invoice data as needed.
2. **Integrating Exported Data with ERP and Financial Systems:**
   - Integrate exported data with ERP and financial systems to provide a unified view of financial data, supporting cash flow management, budgeting, and financial reporting.

- Integration improves data accuracy and provides a single source of truth for financial information.

3. **Creating Consolidated Reports for Executive Summary**:
    - Use exported data to create consolidated reports for executive summaries, focusing on high-level metrics such as total spend, compliance rates, and vendor performance.
    - Executive summaries provide leadership with an overview of accounts payable performance, supporting strategic decision-making.

4. **Performing Advanced Analysis in Business Intelligence Tools**:
    - For advanced analytics, import exported data into business intelligence (BI) tools to perform detailed analysis, visualize trends, and identify deeper insights.
    - BI tools provide enhanced analytics capabilities, allowing organizations to leverage invoice data for strategic planning.

Best Practices for Invoice Reporting and Analytics

Following best practices in reporting and analytics ensures that organizations make the most of SAP

Concur's capabilities, driving strategic insights and process improvements.

1. **Regularly Review and Update Key Metrics**:
   o Periodically review and adjust the metrics tracked in reports to ensure alignment with current business goals and financial priorities.
   o Updated metrics keep reporting relevant, supporting continuous improvement in invoice management.

2. **Involve Stakeholders in Report Design**:
   o Work with stakeholders to determine the most useful data points, customizing reports and dashboards to meet their needs.
   o Stakeholder involvement improves report design, ensuring that reports support decision-making across departments.

3. **Use Visualizations for Quick Interpretation**:
   o Incorporate visualizations such as charts, graphs, and heatmaps to make data easier to interpret and highlight trends or outliers.
   o Visualizations enhance report readability, helping users identify key insights quickly.

4. **Leverage Predictive Analytics for Budgeting**:
    o Use predictive analytics to forecast future spending based on historical data, supporting proactive budget planning and expense management.
    o Forecasting enables finance teams to allocate resources effectively, anticipating needs and managing cash flow.

Common Issues and Troubleshooting in Invoice Reporting

While SAP Concur's reporting tools are user-friendly, some common issues may arise. Here's how to address them effectively.

1. **Data Discrepancies in Reports**:
    o If data discrepancies occur, verify that data mapping and synchronization settings with ERP systems are correct and that all fields align.
    o Resolving discrepancies ensures data integrity and improves report accuracy.
2. **Reports Not Reflecting Real-Time Data**:
    o If reports are not updating in real-time, check the data sync settings and refresh intervals. Adjust the sync frequency to ensure timely data updates.

- Ensuring real-time updates provides accurate insights, supporting timely decisions.

3. **Difficulty Customizing Reports**:
    - For challenges in customizing reports, review SAP Concur's reporting documentation or consult with the support team for guidance on setting filters, adding fields, or adjusting layouts.
    - Customization support enables users to tailor reports to meet specific needs, maximizing reporting effectiveness.

4. **Slow Report Load Times**:
    - If reports are slow to load, try optimizing data filters, reducing the time range, or splitting large reports into smaller sections.
    - Optimized reports improve user experience and reduce time spent waiting for data.

Conclusion

Effective invoice reporting and analytics in SAP Concur provide finance teams with valuable insights into spending patterns, vendor performance, and compliance. By leveraging SAP Concur's reporting tools and following best practices for analysis, organizations can optimize accounts payable processes, enhance financial visibility, and make data-driven decisions.

In the next chapter, we'll cover **Leveraging Mobile Capabilities in SAP Concur**.

This chapter provides a comprehensive guide to using invoice reporting and analytics in SAP Concur.

Chapter 19: Leveraging Mobile Capabilities in SAP Concur

Introduction

SAP Concur's mobile capabilities allow employees to manage expenses, invoices, and approvals on the go, enhancing convenience, efficiency, and productivity. With the SAP Concur mobile app, users can capture receipts, submit expenses, track invoices, and approve reports from their smartphones or tablets, providing flexibility for remote work and business travel. In this chapter, we'll explore the key features of the SAP Concur mobile app, discuss best practices for using mobile capabilities effectively, and outline how organizations can leverage these tools to streamline financial processes.

The Benefits of Mobile Capabilities in SAP Concur

Leveraging SAP Concur's mobile capabilities provides several benefits for both employees and organizations:

1. **Increased Efficiency**: Mobile access enables employees to capture expenses, submit reports, and manage approvals without delays, even while traveling.
2. **Enhanced Data Accuracy**: Real-time data entry reduces the risk of errors and ensures that

expenses are documented accurately as they occur.

3. **Improved Compliance**: Mobile alerts and notifications help employees stay compliant with company policies, reducing the likelihood of missing documentation or late submissions.

4. **Greater Flexibility**: The mobile app supports remote work, allowing employees to manage expenses and invoices from any location.

Key Features of the SAP Concur Mobile App

The SAP Concur mobile app offers a range of features that simplify expense management, invoice processing, and approval workflows. Here are some of the app's most valuable tools:

1. **Receipt Capture**:
   - The mobile app allows users to capture receipts by taking photos with their phone cameras. OCR (Optical Character Recognition) technology automatically extracts key details, such as date, amount, and vendor, from the image.
   - Receipt capture ensures that documentation is recorded immediately, reducing the chance of lost receipts and improving data accuracy.

2. **Expense Report Submission**:
    - o Users can create and submit expense reports directly from the mobile app, selecting expenses, categorizing them, and adding any necessary details.
    - o Mobile submission speeds up the expense reporting process, allowing employees to complete and submit reports on the go, improving turnaround times for reimbursement.
3. **Invoice Management**:
    - o The mobile app provides access to invoices, allowing users to review, track, and approve invoices from their mobile devices.
    - o Mobile invoice management supports timely processing and enables managers to stay on top of approvals even when away from the office.
4. **Approval Workflows**:
    - o Managers can review and approve or reject expense reports and invoices from their mobile devices, streamlining the approval process and preventing delays.
    - o Mobile approvals ensure that workflows progress smoothly, reducing the risk of bottlenecks and supporting timely payments.

5. **Notifications and Alerts**:
   - The app sends push notifications and alerts to remind users of tasks such as pending approvals, overdue expenses, or policy violations.
   - Notifications help employees stay compliant with company policies and reduce the likelihood of missed deadlines.

6. **Mileage Tracking**:
   - The SAP Concur mobile app includes GPS-based mileage tracking, allowing employees to record distance traveled for business purposes accurately.
   - Automated mileage tracking simplifies reimbursement for business travel, ensuring accuracy and reducing manual calculations.

7. **Multi-Currency Support**:
   - For employees traveling internationally, the mobile app supports multiple currencies, allowing expenses to be recorded in the local currency and converted automatically.
   - Multi-currency support simplifies expense reporting for international travel and ensures accurate reimbursements.

Step 1: Setting Up the SAP Concur Mobile App

Setting up the SAP Concur mobile app is a straightforward process. Following these steps ensures that employees can quickly access the app's features and integrate it into their daily workflows.

1. **Downloading the App**:
    - The SAP Concur mobile app is available for both iOS and Android devices. Users can download it from the Apple App Store or Google Play Store.
    - Ensuring that employees use the official app version helps maintain security and compatibility with SAP Concur's desktop application.
2. **Logging in and Setting Up Permissions**:
    - After downloading, users log in with their SAP Concur credentials. For first-time users, administrators may need to verify permissions to access specific features.
    - Configuring permissions ensures that users have access to the tools they need, such as expense entry, approval capabilities, and mileage tracking.
3. **Enabling Notifications**:
    - Encourage users to enable notifications to receive alerts about approvals, report submissions, and reminders for missing receipts.

- Notifications keep employees informed and help prevent missed tasks, enhancing compliance and timely reporting.
4. **Configuring Multi-Currency and Mileage Settings**:
     - Employees who travel internationally should configure multi-currency settings in the app, allowing expenses to be recorded in local currency and converted automatically.
     - For users who frequently log mileage, enable the app's GPS tracking feature to ensure accurate mileage reporting.

Step 2: Capturing Expenses and Receipts on the Go

The SAP Concur mobile app provides tools for capturing expenses and receipts in real time, supporting accurate and timely reporting. Here's how employees can make the most of these features.

1. **Using Receipt Capture for Instant Documentation**:
     - When making a business purchase, employees can immediately use the mobile app's receipt capture function, ensuring that expenses are documented accurately.
     - Immediate documentation reduces the risk of losing receipts and provides a clear

record of business expenses for compliance.

2. **Leveraging OCR for Automated Data Entry**:
   - The app's OCR technology extracts essential details from captured receipts, such as vendor, date, and amount, automatically populating fields in the expense report.
   - OCR reduces the need for manual entry, improving data accuracy and speeding up the expense reporting process.

3. **Organizing Expenses by Category**:
   - After capturing an expense, users can categorize it within the app, selecting from categories such as meals, travel, lodging, or supplies.
   - Categorizing expenses ensures that they align with company policies, supporting accurate reimbursement and budget tracking.

4. **Capturing Multi-Currency Expenses**:
   - For employees traveling internationally, the app allows them to record expenses in the local currency, which SAP Concur automatically converts based on exchange rates.
   - Multi-currency support simplifies expense tracking for international travel, reducing errors in currency conversion.

Step 3: Submitting Expense Reports and Managing Invoices

The SAP Concur mobile app enables employees to submit expense reports and track invoices while on the move, reducing delays in reimbursement and payment processing.

1. **Creating and Submitting Expense Reports**:
    o Employees can create expense reports directly within the mobile app, adding individual expenses, categorizing them, and including any necessary comments or justifications.
    o Submitting reports from a mobile device streamlines the process, allowing employees to submit reports promptly, reducing processing times.
2. **Reviewing and Approving Invoices**:
    o Managers can access and review invoices from their mobile devices, approving or rejecting them based on company policies and budget considerations.
    o Mobile approvals prevent bottlenecks in the invoice workflow, ensuring timely payments to vendors and supporting efficient accounts payable processes.
3. **Tracking Report and Invoice Status**:
    o Users can monitor the status of their submitted expense reports and invoices,

checking whether they are awaiting approval, approved, or paid.
- ○ Real-time status tracking provides transparency, allowing employees and managers to stay updated on pending tasks.

4. **Handling Policy Violations and Exceptions**:
   - ○ The app flags any expenses that fall outside policy guidelines, prompting users to review and adjust entries if needed. Managers can also review and approve exceptions if they are justified.
   - ○ Managing policy violations on the go supports compliance and minimizes delays in processing reports or invoices with exceptions.

Step 4: Leveraging Notifications and Alerts for Timely Actions

Notifications and alerts in the SAP Concur mobile app keep employees informed of critical actions, deadlines, and approvals. Leveraging these tools helps ensure timely task completion and compliance.

1. **Enabling Notifications for Approvals and Pending Actions**:
   - ○ Configure notifications to alert users of pending approvals, report submissions, and receipts that require documentation.

- Notifications prompt timely actions, reducing delays and ensuring that tasks are completed within required timelines.

2. **Setting Up Policy Violation Alerts:**
   - Users receive alerts for any expenses that violate company policy, allowing them to address issues immediately by providing justifications or adjusting entries.
   - Policy alerts help employees stay compliant and ensure that expenses meet organizational standards.

3. **Receiving Reminders for Incomplete Reports:**
   - For incomplete reports, the app sends reminders to users to attach missing receipts, add explanations for policy exceptions, or complete other necessary steps.
   - Reminders improve compliance by helping employees avoid missed documentation and ensuring that all requirements are met before submission.

4. **Monitoring Payment Notifications:**
   - Once expenses or invoices are processed for payment, users receive notifications confirming the status, providing transparency into reimbursement and payment timelines.
   - Payment notifications keep users informed, minimizing follow-up inquiries

and improving satisfaction with the accounts payable process.

Step 5: Best Practices for Using the SAP Concur Mobile App

Following best practices for using the SAP Concur mobile app ensures that employees maximize its capabilities and maintain compliance with company policies.

1. **Capture Receipts Immediately**:
   - Encourage employees to capture receipts as soon as expenses occur, ensuring that documentation is accurate and timely.
   - Immediate receipt capture reduces the risk of missing receipts and supports accurate reporting.
2. **Use OCR to Reduce Manual Entry**:
   - Take advantage of the app's OCR functionality to minimize manual data entry, improving efficiency and reducing errors.
   - OCR automation allows employees to complete reports faster, saving time and enhancing data accuracy.
3. **Set Up Notifications for Key Tasks**:
   - Enable notifications for essential tasks, such as pending approvals and policy

violations, to ensure timely completion and compliance.

- o Notifications keep users on track, minimizing the risk of missed tasks and improving workflow efficiency.

4. **Keep the App Updated for Security and Performance**:
   - o Regularly update the SAP Concur mobile app to access the latest features, performance enhancements, and security patches.
   - o Keeping the app updated ensures optimal functionality and protects against potential security vulnerabilities.

5. **Review Reports and Invoices Before Submission**:
   - o Encourage users to review their reports and invoices for completeness, accuracy, and policy compliance before submission, reducing the likelihood of rejections.
   - o Thorough review ensures compliance with company policies and supports a smoother approval process.

Troubleshooting Common Issues in the SAP Concur Mobile App

While the SAP Concur mobile app is designed to be user-friendly, occasional issues may arise. Here are solutions to some common problems:

1. **App Crashes or Freezes**:
   - If the app crashes or freezes, try closing it and reopening, or restarting the device. Ensure the app is updated to the latest version.
   - Regular updates improve app performance and reduce the likelihood of technical issues.
2. **Poor OCR Accuracy**:
   - If OCR fails to extract data accurately, ensure the receipt image is clear, properly aligned, and well-lit. Re-take the photo if necessary.
   - Clear images improve OCR accuracy, supporting accurate data extraction for expense reporting.
3. **Delayed Notifications**:
   - If notifications are delayed, check device notification settings to ensure that alerts for the SAP Concur app are enabled.
   - Proper notification settings help employees receive timely alerts for approvals and pending actions.

4. **Difficulty Logging In**:
   - For login issues, verify the credentials and check the network connection. If the problem persists, reset the password or contact SAP Concur support.
   - Ensuring access to the app allows employees to use mobile capabilities effectively.

Conclusion

The SAP Concur mobile app enhances convenience and efficiency for expense management, invoice processing, and approval workflows. By leveraging its mobile capabilities, employees can capture receipts, track invoices, and complete approvals on the go, supporting timely task completion and streamlined financial processes.

In the next chapter, we will explore **Best Practices for Optimizing SAP Concur**.

This chapter provides a comprehensive guide to leveraging SAP Concur's mobile capabilities for improved expense and invoice management.

Chapter 20: Best Practices for Optimizing SAP Concur

Introduction

Optimizing SAP Concur involves refining processes, leveraging automation, and ensuring that the platform aligns with organizational goals. By following best practices for setup, data management, compliance, and user engagement, organizations can maximize the benefits of SAP Concur, streamlining expense and invoice workflows while reducing costs and improving data accuracy. This chapter provides a comprehensive guide to best practices for optimizing SAP Concur, ensuring that organizations get the most from their investment.

The Benefits of Optimizing SAP Concur

Implementing best practices for SAP Concur drives several critical benefits:

1. **Increased Efficiency**: Streamlined processes reduce manual tasks, saving time for employees and accounts payable teams.
2. **Enhanced Compliance**: Optimized policies and automated checks support adherence to organizational standards and regulatory requirements.

3. **Cost Control**: By tracking spending, managing vendor relationships, and enforcing policies, organizations can better control expenses.
4. **Improved Data Accuracy**: Consistent data management practices reduce errors, supporting accurate reporting and audit readiness.
5. **Higher User Engagement**: Training, mobile accessibility, and ease of use encourage employee participation, ensuring compliance and reducing processing times.

Key Areas for Optimization in SAP Concur

Optimization efforts in SAP Concur can be divided into several focus areas: configuration, automation, user engagement, data management, and reporting. Each area contributes to a more efficient, compliant, and data-driven expense and invoice management process.

1. **Configuration**: Setting up the platform to meet organizational requirements, from defining expense categories to configuring approval workflows.
2. **Automation**: Leveraging automated workflows, notifications, and data capture to reduce manual intervention and streamline processes.
3. **User Engagement and Training**: Ensuring that employees understand how to use SAP Concur effectively, from mobile app usage to compliance with expense policies.

4. **Data Management and Accuracy**: Maintaining accurate and up-to-date data within SAP Concur, including vendor information, expense categories, and reporting structures.
5. **Analytics and Reporting**: Using data insights to improve decision-making, track compliance, and refine expense policies based on trends.

Step 1: Optimizing Configuration and Workflow Setup

A well-configured SAP Concur platform is the foundation of an efficient expense and invoice management system. Focusing on configuration ensures that SAP Concur aligns with the organization's unique needs and policies.

1. **Define Expense Categories and Policies**:
   o Create detailed expense categories, such as travel, meals, lodging, and office supplies, tailored to the organization's spending patterns.
   o Defining clear categories and policies supports accurate tracking, simplifies reporting, and ensures that employees follow organizational guidelines.
2. **Customize Approval Workflows**:
   o Set up approval workflows based on factors such as expense amount, department, or specific categories. For

example, high-value expenses may require additional approvals.

- o Custom workflows reduce bottlenecks and ensure that each expense receives the appropriate level of scrutiny, supporting compliance and efficiency.

3. **Establish Multi-Currency and International Settings**:
   - o For organizations with international employees, configure multi-currency options and set up foreign exchange rate conversions to ensure accurate expense tracking.
   - o Multi-currency settings streamline reporting for international expenses, improving accuracy in expense records and simplifying reimbursement.

4. **Enable Conditional Approval for Policy Exceptions**:
   - o Configure workflows to handle exceptions, such as policy violations or unusual expenses, by routing them to senior management for review.
   - o Conditional approval workflows add flexibility while maintaining control over out-of-policy expenses.

5. **Automate Compliance Checks**:
   - o Set up automated policy checks to flag expenses that fall outside approved

guidelines, such as those exceeding category limits or missing receipts.
- o Automated compliance checks ensure policy adherence while reducing the workload on managers, enabling faster approvals and compliance enforcement.

Step 2: Leveraging Automation to Reduce Manual Work

Automation within SAP Concur saves time and reduces errors by minimizing manual intervention. By automating processes, organizations can streamline approvals, improve data accuracy, and ensure that tasks are completed on time.

1. **Use OCR for Automated Receipt Capture**:
   - o Encourage employees to use the mobile app's OCR feature to capture receipts, allowing the system to automatically extract relevant data.
   - o OCR reduces manual entry, improving data accuracy and saving time for employees, especially those frequently on the move.
2. **Schedule Automated Notifications and Reminders**:
   - o Set up automated reminders for tasks such as pending approvals, missing

receipts, and overdue expense reports to keep workflows on track.

- o Notifications help employees and managers stay informed, ensuring that tasks are completed in a timely manner and reducing processing delays.

3. **Automate Recurring Expenses**:
   - o For routine or predictable expenses, such as monthly subscriptions, use automation to streamline reporting and avoid repetitive data entry.
   - o Automating recurring expenses reduces the administrative burden on employees and ensures consistent documentation.

4. **Integrate with ERP and Financial Systems**:
   - o Integrate SAP Concur with the organization's ERP or accounting system to automate data transfers, reducing the need for manual data entry and ensuring accurate financial reporting.
   - o Integration with ERP systems provides a unified view of financial data, improving visibility into expenses and supporting more accurate budgeting and planning.

5. **Implement Multi-Level Approval Automation**:
   - o For complex workflows, automate the routing of expenses based on approval thresholds. For instance, expenses over a specified amount automatically move to a higher-level approver.

- Multi-level automation streamlines approvals for high-value transactions, reducing bottlenecks and ensuring proper oversight.

Step 3: Enhancing User Engagement and Training

Employee engagement is key to successful adoption of SAP Concur. Training and encouraging effective use of the platform improves compliance, reduces errors, and enhances productivity.

1. **Provide Comprehensive Training for New Users**:
   - Offer onboarding sessions for new users, covering basic functions such as capturing receipts, submitting reports, and understanding expense policies.
   - Comprehensive training ensures that employees understand how to use SAP Concur efficiently and comply with organizational guidelines.
2. **Encourage Mobile App Usage for Convenience**:
   - Promote the use of the SAP Concur mobile app, especially for employees who travel frequently or work remotely. Highlight features such as receipt capture, mileage tracking, and expense submission.

- Mobile access increases convenience, making it easier for employees to record expenses accurately and on time.

3. **Offer Ongoing Policy Updates and Refresher Training**:
   - Regularly update employees on any changes to expense policies, spending limits, or compliance requirements. Offer refresher training to reinforce correct usage.
   - Keeping employees informed of policy updates improves compliance and reduces the risk of policy violations.

4. **Set Up User Support and Troubleshooting Resources**:
   - Provide employees with access to resources such as FAQs, video tutorials, and support contacts to assist with common issues.
   - Readily available support encourages employees to use SAP Concur confidently and reduces the likelihood of errors in expense reporting.

5. **Incentivize Compliance with Policies**:
   - Recognize or reward employees who consistently follow expense policies and submit accurate reports, reinforcing the importance of compliance.

- Incentives encourage proper use of SAP Concur and help establish a culture of compliance within the organization.

Step 4: Maintaining Accurate Data and Vendor Management

Accurate data is essential for effective expense management and reporting. By maintaining up-to-date information in SAP Concur, organizations improve reporting accuracy, support audit readiness, and enhance vendor relationships.

1. **Regularly Update Vendor Information**:
   - Keep vendor profiles current, including details such as contact information, payment terms, and preferred currency.
   - Accurate vendor information supports timely payments, improves vendor relationships, and enhances data integrity.
2. **Ensure Consistency in Expense Categories and GL Codes**:
   - Review and standardize expense categories, GL (General Ledger) codes, and reporting structures to maintain consistency across departments.
   - Standardization ensures that expense data aligns with accounting

requirements, simplifying reconciliation and financial reporting.

3. **Review Data Mapping for Integrated Systems**:
   - For organizations that integrate SAP Concur with ERP or financial systems, periodically review data mapping to ensure consistency between systems.
   - Accurate data mapping improves data integrity, reducing discrepancies and enhancing the quality of financial records.

4. **Validate Multi-Currency Data**:
   - For global organizations, validate multi-currency settings to ensure accurate exchange rates and conversions in expense records.
   - Proper multi-currency data management simplifies international reporting and supports accurate reimbursement for employees.

5. **Conduct Regular Data Audits**:
   - Periodically audit expense and vendor data in SAP Concur to verify accuracy, identify any inconsistencies, and address data entry errors.
   - Regular audits improve data quality, support audit readiness, and ensure that records align with organizational standards.

Step 5: Leveraging Analytics and Reporting for Strategic Insights

SAP Concur's reporting and analytics tools provide valuable insights into spending patterns, compliance trends, and process efficiency. Leveraging these insights supports data-driven decision-making and continuous improvement.

1. **Track Spending by Department and Category**:
   - Use reports to monitor spending across departments and expense categories, identifying areas of high expenditure and potential cost savings.
   - Department and category insights enable better budget allocation and help identify areas where spending controls may be needed.
2. **Monitor Compliance with Policy Reports**:
   - Regularly review policy compliance reports to track adherence to expense policies and identify any frequent violations.
   - Compliance monitoring ensures that policies are enforced effectively, supporting audit readiness and reducing out-of-policy expenses.

3. **Analyze Approval Times and Workflow Bottlenecks**:
    - o Track approval times for expense reports and invoices to identify delays in the workflow. Address any bottlenecks to improve processing efficiency.
    - o Workflow analysis supports smoother approval processes and reduces turnaround time for reimbursements and payments.
4. **Identify High-Value Vendors and Spending Trends**:
    - o Use vendor reports to track spending by supplier, helping identify high-value vendors and assess performance. Use this data to negotiate better terms or consolidate vendors.
    - o Vendor insights improve supplier management and support cost-effective purchasing decisions.
5. **Leverage Predictive Analytics for Budgeting**:
    - o Use historical spending data to forecast future expenses, supporting proactive budgeting and financial planning.
    - o Predictive analytics provide valuable insights for decision-makers, helping organizations allocate resources effectively and manage cash flow.

Best Practices for Long-Term Optimization

Following best practices over the long term helps organizations maintain an efficient, compliant, and user-friendly SAP Concur environment that evolves with business needs.

1. **Conduct Periodic System Reviews**:
   - Regularly review SAP Concur settings, policies, and workflows to ensure they align with current organizational goals and regulatory requirements.
   - Periodic reviews ensure that SAP Concur remains optimized as business needs evolve, supporting long-term efficiency.
2. **Solicit Feedback from Users**:
   - Gather feedback from employees and managers on their experience with SAP Concur, using it to make targeted improvements to the platform.
   - User feedback provides insights into potential enhancements, ensuring the platform meets user needs and encourages engagement.
3. **Stay Updated on SAP Concur Enhancements**:
   - Keep up with SAP Concur's latest features, updates, and best practices, as new tools may enhance efficiency or improve compliance.

- o Staying informed of SAP Concur developments allows organizations to continually enhance their use of the platform.
4. **Reinforce Compliance Culture**:
   - o Encourage a culture of compliance by promoting transparency, providing regular training, and recognizing adherence to policies.
   - o A compliance-focused culture ensures that employees use SAP Concur responsibly, reducing policy violations and audit risks.
5. **Optimize for Scalability and Growth**:
   - o Configure SAP Concur to support future growth, allowing for the addition of new departments, currencies, or international users.
   - o Scalable configurations ensure that SAP Concur continues to meet organizational needs as the business expands.

Conclusion

Optimizing SAP Concur is a continuous process that requires attention to configuration, automation, user engagement, data accuracy, and strategic analysis. By implementing best practices across these areas, organizations can maximize the platform's efficiency, support compliance, and drive informed decision-making. As organizations continue to evolve, maintaining an optimized SAP Concur environment ensures that expense and invoice management processes remain agile, accurate, and aligned with business goals.

This chapter concludes the best practices for optimizing SAP Concur, equipping organizations to enhance their expense and invoice management effectively.

www.ingramcontent.com/pod-product-compliance
Lightning Source LLC
LaVergne TN
LVHW081753050326
832903LV00027B/1924